The
Establishment
and Limits *of*
Civil
Government

The Establishment *and* Limits *of* Civil Government

AN EXPOSITION OF ROMANS 13:1–7

JAMES M. WILLSON

Foreword by
Gary DeMar

American Vision Press
POWDER SPRINGS, GEORGIA

The Establishment and Limits of Civil Government
An Exposition of Romans 13:1–7
by James M. Willson

Originally published in 1853 as:
Civil Government: An Exposition of Romans XIII. 1–7

Copyright © 2009 *The American Vision, Inc.*
The American Vision, Inc.
3150–A Florence Road
Powder Springs, Georgia 30127-5385
www.AmericanVision.org
1-800-628-9460

Printed in the United States of America.

Cover design by Luis Lovelace
Typesetting by Adam Stiles & Luis Lovelace

ISBN 10: 0-915815-54-0
ISBN 13: 978-0-915815-54-8

Contents

JAMES M. WILLSON

James McLeod Willson was born near Elizabeth, Allegheny County, Pennsylvania on November 17, 1809. He graduated from Union College in 1829. He studied theology under the direction of his father, James R. Willson, and was licensed by the Presbytery, June 5, 1834. He was ordained by the same Presbytery, and installed pastor of the First congregation of Philadelphia, November 27, 1834. He was elected Professor of Theology in the Allegheny Seminary, May 31, 1859. He authored numerous pamphlets and books, including *Bible Magistracy: or Christ's Dominion Over the Nations: With an Examination of the Civil Institutions of the United States*; *An Essay on Submission to the Powers that Be*; *Witnessing: or the Distinct Denomination Position of the Reformed Presbyterian Church Right and Necessary*. He died at his residence in Allegheny, August 31, 1866.

FOREWORD
by
Gary DeMar

"It can't happen here!" How many times have we heard this claim? But it can happen here. Many will tell you that it is happening here. It seems that almost on a daily basis we are losing our rights, an endowment from the Creator, as the Declaration of Independence states. Some even make the case that there is a direct assault on the Christian religion *because* it puts limits on governments and establishes moral boundaries. To grow the State means that biblical law must be reinterpreted or made to disappear altogether. Relegating God to a distant corner of the universe or redefining and remaking Him in the image of the politically empowered emboldens governments to "do what they will"[1] without any regard to any fixed moral standard outside of man and governments. In pre-Nazi Germany, many Christians were under the false assumption that they had to go along with whatever their civil rulers demanded no matter how contrary their actions were in relation to God's law. A similar thing is happening among today's Christians in America.

A two-kingdom approach to society had been taught since the time of Augustine and reinforced by the work of Martin

Luther. Two-kingdom social theory teaches that "heavenly things" are directed exclusively by God's redemptive grace through Special Revelation while "earthly things" are formulated by God's common grace through Natural Revelation. In this ideal but naïve world, believers and unbelievers, because they are created in the image of God, can work together to construct society using common-ground features found in Natural Revelation and guided by reason. As long as most people believed in God, such a world was theoretically possible since Natural Revelation was interpreted, either consciously or unconsciously, by Special Revelation, the Bible.

This all changed in 1859 with the publication of Charles Darwin's *On the Origin of Species*. Evolution killed Special Revelation, common grace, Natural Revelation, and the belief that there is a common humanity created in the image of God. In time, as Francis Schaeffer put it, nature, that which is known through reason, began to "eat up grace,"[2] that which is known through revelation.[3] Special Revelation was dismissed as impossible in a purely materialistic and evolving cosmos. In a 1948 article in *The Bible Today*, Schaeffer describes what an individual who is consistent with his nature-only worldview is left with: "If the unsaved man was consistent he would be an atheist in religion, an irrationalist in philosophy (including a complete uncertainty concerning 'natural laws'), and completely a-moral in the widest sense."[4] There is no way to appeal to a two-kingdom approach given the assumptions of modern-day atheistic science.

This real shift in worldview thinking is expressed dramatically in the film *The Dark Knight* (2008) when Bruce Wayne (Christian Bale) tells Alfred (Michael Cain) that criminals are "not complicated," we just need to find out what The Joker wants. In a world where there is general agreement that there is an acknowledged universal moral order, the actions of criminals have always made sense. Even criminals knew that what they were doing was wrong. But there's something different about The Joker. He operates from a different point of view, an anti-point of view. Alfred tells Bruce that "some men just want to watch the world burn." "There is no ultimate purpose to his mayhem; he delights in it for its own sake, as is evident in one particularly chilling scene in which Batman tries to beat him into revealing his plans. As The Joker cackles with glee at the pain, he taunts Batman, 'you have nothing to frighten me with.'"[5] The Joker lives in a world that is beyond good and evil. There cannot be a two-kingdom approach for those who live in The Joker's world, and there are an increasing number of Jokers out there if statistics are accurate. Richard Dawkins is up front with his claim that "Darwin made it possible to be an intellectually fulfilled atheist."[6] It can also be said that Darwin made it possible to be an intellectually fulfilled nihilist, living "beyond good and evil."[7]

The two-kingdom approach to Christian social theory was used to great advantage by Adolf Hitler. He knew that many Christians believed that the particulars of their religious worldview only applied to spiritual things. Civil government operated in the secular realm where natural revelation was the standard. "A Majority within the state church (known as the 'German Christians') unwittingly or otherwise embraced the new national religion, founded not on the Word of God but on the divine will allegedly embedded in the natural order. Emerging from this fatal exchange came a semi-Christian natural religion (some would say a new paganism) in which the church became a servile instrument of Nazi policy...."[8] Hitler knew that there was a lot he could get away with because a majority of Christians did not believe that it was permissible to bring the Bible to bear in realms they considered to be outside its self-imposed jurisdiction. Politics was considered neutral territory. Whoever was in power was God's minister whether he did good or evil. Richard V. Pierard comments:

> In the nineteenth century ... German Lutherans made a strong bifurcation between the realm of public and private concerns.... Religion was the domain of the inner personal life, while the institutional and external, the public, so to speak, belonged to the worldly power. Redemption was exclusively the province of the church, while the law, determinative for external conduct of human affairs, was solely the province of the state. Religion was a private matter that concerned itself with the personal and moral development of the individual. The external order—nature, scientific knowledge, statecraft—operated on the basis of its own internal logic and discernable laws.[9]

For decades before the rise of Hitler, Christians were subjected to arguments like the following from pastors and theologians based on the two-kingdom theory:

- "The Gospel has absolutely nothing to do with outward existence but only with eternal life, not with external orders and institutions which could come in conflict with the secular orders but only with the heart and its relationship with God."[10]

- "The Gospel frees us from this world, frees us from all questions of this world, frees us inwardly, also from the questions of public life, also from the social question. Christianity has no answer to these questions."[11]

- Once the Christian understands the moral significance of the state, Wilhelm Hermann declared in 1913, "he will consider obedience to the government to be the highest vocation within the state. For the authority of the state on the whole, resting as it does upon authority of the government, is more important than the elimination of any shortcomings which it might have.... For the person who is inwardly free, it is more important [that] the state preserve its historical continuity than that he obtain justice for himself."[12]

While many Christians might have been opposed to Nazi policies at a *personal* level, they had been conditioned to believe—because they were Christians living in two kingdoms operating with two sets of standards—that they could not do anything about these rapidly implemented policies at a *political* level. Much of their thinking was shaped by a misreading of Romans 13 and a misapplication of Matthew 22:21 where Jesus says "Render unto Caesar the things that are Caesar's." As with all authority, there are limits, including limits on civil government. We know this only from the Bible. It might also help to realize that we do not live under Caesar. Our civil rulers took an oath to uphold the Constitution which is the "supreme law of the land." Neither the president nor the members of Congress are Caesar. If we have a "Caesar," it is the United States Constitution. But even the Constitution recognizes its own limits and the right of the people to (1) express their grievances, (2) vote corrupt and oath-breaking rulers out of office, and (3) change existing laws through an amendment process.

Paul McGuire, an evangelical syndicated talk-show host out of Los Angeles explains why so many Christians are indifferent to a culture beyond the personal and keep their distance from politics and social issues:

> The root is theological and it goes back to Francis Schaeffer's comments about the Christian culture being pietistic or super-spiritual.[13] The Christian culture does not believe that Jesus is lord of all of life. The evangelical culture believes the nonbiblical idea that Jesus is only lord of Bible study, prayer, and church attendance, and anything outside of that is not really spiritual.[14]

We've seen such attitudes before. Over time, churches in Nazi German were "confined as far as possible to the performance of narrowly religious functions, and even within this narrow sphere were subjected to as many hindrances as the Nazis dared to impose." This is the evaluation of a 1945 report published by the Office of Strategic Services (OSS), the precursor to the CIA. It was called *The Nazi Master Plan: The Persecution of the Christian Churches* and was prepared for the War Crimes Staff. It offered the following summary: "This study describes, with illustrative factual evidence, Nazi purposes, policies and methods of persecuting the Christian Churches in Germany and occupied Europe."

Where did the strategic plan begin? "Implementation of this objective started with the curtailment of religious instruction in the primary and secondary schools with the squeezing of the religious periods into inconvenient hours, with Nazi propaganda among the teachers in order to induce them to refuse the teaching of religion, with vetoing of ... religious text books, and finally with substituting [a] Nazi *Weltanschauung* [worldview] and 'German faith' for Christian religious denominational instruction.... At the time of the outbreak of the war ... religious instruction had practically disappeared from Germany's primary schools." Does any of this sound familiar? This is a perfect description of our nation's education system with the only difference being that a materialistic worldview and "secular" faith have replaced the once Christian worldview that served as the foundation of education in America.

The next step was to neutralize the impact that churches would have on politics. "Under the pretext that the Churches themselves were interfering in political and state matters, [the Nazis] would deprive the Churches, step by step, of all opportunity to affect German public life." How often do we hear that the "separation between church and state" means that churches must remain silent on social and political issues, that pastors cannot use their pulpits (unless they're liberal) to influence legislation?

When Martin Niemoeller used his pulpit to expose Adolf Hitler's radical politics, "He knew every word spoken was reported by Nazi spies and secret agents."[15] Leo Stein describes in his book *I Was in Hell with Niemoeller* how the Gestapo gathered evidence against Niemoeller:

> Now, the charge against Niemoeller was based entirely on his sermons, which the Gestapo agents had taken down stenographically. But in none of his sermons did Pastor Niemoeller exhort his congregation to overthrow the Nazi regime. He merely raised his voice against some of the Nazi policies, particularly the policy directed against the Church. He had even refrained from criticizing the Nazi government itself or any of its personnel. Under the former government his sermons would have been construed only as an exercise of the right of free speech. Now, however, written laws, no matter how

explicitly they were worded, were subjected to the interpretation of the judges.[16]

In a June 27, 1937 sermon, Niemoeller made it clear to those in attendance had a sacred duty to speak out on the evils of the Nazi regime no matter what the consequences: "We have no more thought of using our own powers to escape the arm of the authorities than had the Apostles of old. No more are we ready to keep silent at man's behest when God commands us to speak. For it is, and must remain, the case that we must obey God rather than man."[17] A few days later, he was arrested. His crime? "Abuse of the pulpit."

The "Special Courts" set up by the Nazis made claims against pastors who spoke out against Hitler's policies. Niemoeller was not the only one singled out by the Gestapo. "Some 807 other pastors and leading laymen of the 'Confessional Church' were arrested in 1937, and hundreds more in the next couple of years."[18] A group of Confessional Churches in Germany, founded by Pastor Niemoeller and other Protestant ministers, drew up a proclamation to confront the political changes taking place in Germany that threatened the people "with a deadly danger. The danger lies in a new religion," the proclamation declared. "The church has by order of its Master to see to it that in our people Christ is given the honor that is proper to the Judge of the world.... The First Commandment says 'Thou shalt have no other gods before me.' The new religion is a rejection of the First Commandment."[19] Five hundred pastors who read the proclamation from their pulpits were arrested.

The Bible tells us that civil rulers are *ministers of God*. The Greek word translated "ministers" is the same word used to describe "ministers" in a church and is often translated as "deacon" or "servant." Both serve as God's servants toward the people within their jurisdictions, one civil (State) and the other ecclesiastical (Church). It is unbiblical to assume that civil rulers are autonomous, that they can legitimately rule independent of God's limiting authority of them. It is a serious mistake to take Paul's instructions in Romans 13 and claim that civil rulers cannot be challenged by the citizenry in their actions. James Willson makes the point in his book *The Establishment and Limits of Civil Government*,[20] "For surely none but an atheist can deliberately affirm that even the law of the land can set aside, weaken or nullify the authority of the law of God. To the best government, obedience can be yielded only in things lawful; for there is a 'higher law' to which rulers and subjects are alike amenable."[21]

One of the reasons King James I wanted a new English translation of the Bible was because he did not like some of the notes found in the Geneva Bible. Some of the notes condemned rulers who acted contrary to God's Word in terms of absolute power. For example, a marginal note for Exodus 1:19 stated that the Hebrew midwives were correct to disobey the Egyptian king's order to kill the Hebrew babies. King James reasoned that if it was legitimate to oppose a ruler in one case, then it might be legitimate to oppose him in others.

Notice the use of "governing authorities" in Romans 13:1; there are many. Even Rome had governors and other civil officials. Our own system of civil government follows the biblical model of multiple civil rulers with county, state, and national authorities. American civil government was designed to be decentralized and limited at all levels. We have a *United* States Constitution and 50 *state* constitutions. It's unfortunate that as a nation we have turned unwarranted and unconstitutional authority over to the national government to the exclusion of state and county governments.

Civil authorities are to rule in terms of "good and evil." There is no room for tyranny in these words. Those who rule are bound by the same laws as the rest of us. That's why there is no divine right of kings in the Bible. The Hebrew midwives disobeyed an order from Pharaoh (Ex. 1:17). The prophet Nathan challenged King David to do right (2 Sam. 12). Daniel was not a revolutionary when he opposed the king's law (Dan. 6). John the Baptist rebuked King Herod for his sexual sins (Matt. 14:3–5). Jesus even called him a "fox" (Luke 13:32). Peter continued to preach, obeying God rather than man, even though he was commanded to stop by the authorities of his day (Acts 5:29). Paul used his Roman citizenship to challenge the Roman Empire (Acts 22:25–30. Paul spent a great deal of time in prison because he was seen as a threat to the Empire.

To obey Romans 13 is to call our civil officials to uphold their oath of office, an oath that nearly all of them took by affirming "So help me God!" Once a civil ruler takes political office, he has the "power of the sword," that is, he has civil authority and the claim of governmental legitimacy to enforce the law by the use of civil sanctions. By not limiting the power of civil government with our voices and votes, we give a free hand to officials to act independent of any human restraint to tax our income at any level, confiscate our property, send our children to war, and even to kill us if a crime is deemed egregious enough. And who gets to determine what constitutes a crime? Civil rulers alone unless they are held accountable for their actions by the electorate, but only an informed electorate is in the position to act as a brake on the unbridled power of the State.

Foreword

James Willson's study of Romans 13, *The Establishment and Limits of Civil Government,* is needed more than ever in our day. What's most helpful about it is that it was written in a time that does not muddy the principles by the highly charged politics of our day. There are no current or recently passed politicians named. He sticks to principles based on the biblical record. If we are to save our Republic, then we are bound to heed his instruction and warnings as they are derived from God's Word.

Notes

1. "Do what thou wilt shall be the whole of the Law." This is the philosophy of *Thelema* based on the writings of English occultist Aleister Crowley (1875–1947) as described in his *Book of the Law*. *Thelema* is the English transliteration of the Koine Greek noun θελημα ("will") from the verb θελω ("to will, wish, purpose"). According to Crowly, "Every man and every woman is not only a part of God, but the Ultimate God…. There are no 'standards of Right.' Ethics is balderdash. Each Star must go on its own orbit. To hell with 'moral principle'; there is no such thing. That is a herd-delusion, and makes men cattle." (Aleister Crowley, *The Old and New Commentaries to Liber AL vel Legis*). Crowley taught a form of heightened spirituality for the enlightened who had found their own inner god.

2. This theme is developed by Schaeffer in *Escape From Reason* in *The Complete Works of Francis A. Schaeffer: A Christian Worldview,* 5 vols., 2nd ed. (Wheaton, IL: Crossway Books, 1982), 1:207–270.

3. Nature eating up grace happened in his own family as evidenced in the publication of his son's book *Crazy for God: How I Grew Up as One of the Elect, Helped Found the Religious Right, and Lived to Take all (or Most All) of it Back* (2007).

4. Francis A. Schaeffer, "A Review of a Review," *The Bible Today* (October 1948).

5. Thomas S. Hibbs, "Christopher Nolan's Achievement: *Dark Night,*" *First Things* (July 22, 2008)

6. Richard Dawkins, *The Blind Watchmaker: Why the Evidence of Evolution Reveals a Universe Without Design* (New York: W.W. Norton & Co., 1986), 6.

7. The title of the book by the German philosopher Friedrich Nietzsche first published in 1886.

8. Bruce A. Demarest, *General Revelation: Historical Views and Contemporary Issues* (Grand Rapids, MI: Zondervan/Academie, 1982), 15.

9. Richard V. Pierard, "Why Did Protestants Welcome Hitler?," *Fides et Historia*, X:2 (Spring 1978), 13.

10. Christian Ernst Luthard (1867). Quoted by Pierard from Karl H. Hertz, *Two Kingdoms and One World: A Sourcebook in Christian Ethics* (Minneapolis: Augusburg, 1976), 83.

11. Quoted in Hertz, *Two Kingdoms and One World: A Sourcebook in Christian Ethics*, 87.

12. Quoted in Hertz, *Two Kingdoms and One World: A Sourcebook in Christian Ethics*, 91.

13. Schaeffer, *The New Super-Spirituality* in *The Complete Works of Francis A. Schaeffer*, 3:383–401.

14. Quoted in Mark Bergin, "Air Supply," *World* (May 9, 2009), 37. It's unfortunate that McGuire holds to a prophetic position that helps Christians justify their "super-spiritual" perspective. See Gary DeMar, *Last Days Madness, Is Jesus Coming Soon?*, and *Why the End of the World is Not in Your Future* published by American Vision: www.AmericanVision.com

15. Basil Miller, *Martin Niemoeller: Hero of the Concentration Camp*, 5th ed. (Grand Rapids, MI: Zondervan, 1942), 112.

16. Leo Stein, *I Was in Hell with Niemoeller* (New York: Fleming H. Revell, 1942), 175.

17. Quoted in William L. Shirer, *The Rise and Fall of the Third Reich* (New York: Simon and Schuster, 1960), 239.

18. Shirer, *The Rise and Fall of the Third Reich*, 239.

19. Quoted in Eugene Davidson, *The Trials of the Germans: An Account of the Twenty-Two Defendants before the International Military Tribunal at Nuremberg* (Columbia, MO: University of Missouri Press, [1966] 1997), 275.

20. James Willson's *The Establishment and Limits of Civil Government: An Exposition of Romans 13:1–7* (Powder Springs, GA: American Vision, 2009) was originally published in 1853 as *Civil Government: An Exposition of Romans XIII. 1–7*.

21. Willson, *The Establishment and Limits of Civil Government*, 22.

INTRODUCTION

by

Archie P. Jones, Ph.D

It is difficult to imagine a subject of more importance to Christians today than the subject of this great book, *The Establishment and Limits of Civil Government: An Exposition of Romans 13:1–7.* For civil government, as the word of God itself tells us in the passage analyzed so ably by James M. Willson, is an institution ordained by God to serve Him as His ministry for His ethical purposes as they relate to *civil* government: to wield the power of the sword to punish, restrain those who do evil, and to protect and give praise to those who do that which is good. And as this careful, thoughtful explication of this key New Testament passage on the ministry of civil government is republished after nearly 160 years, Christians throughout the world are beset by civil governments which function more as ministries of Satan than as ministries of the living God. Moreover, Americans, the beneficiaries of a great (though not perfect) tradition of Christian civil government and law [1], have been faced for some time with a civil government that has not only been dedicated to overturning virtually all of the principles of its own Constitution but has also committed, in the name of an anti-biblical system of "morality" and unaccountable "rights," to violating every God-given principle of civil government, law, liberty and justice.

As a people, we deserve such an ungodly civil government, for we have long since turned from anything like a fully biblical faith in God, and so also from a biblical understanding of the nature and purposes of His ministry of civil government and from obedience to His commandments. How we got ourselves into such a position is a long, complicated story. But it can be summarized in Americans' following after modern man-centered thought. This was done by crafty men seizing the opportunities presented by historical circumstances to subvert our Constitution, centralize our governmental system, pervert our laws, and destroy our liberty in the name of autonomous amoral "freedom." Christians share in the guilt since many have abandoned the Bible as the whole counsel of God as fully inspired and authoritatively applicable to all areas of thought and life—including God's ministry of civil government. Modern man-centered thought is self-consciously in rebellion against God, the Bible, Christianity, and biblical ethics. American man-centered intellectuals' thinking has generally followed European thought, lagging a decade or more behind European intellectual fashions for most of our history. Humanistic American thought has followed European humanistic thought from rationalism (faith in the infallibility of man's unaided reason), from the 19th through the early 20th centuries; to empiricism (faith in the scientific method), from the mid-19th through the 20th centuries; to irrationalism (belief that the world and life are meaningless and standardless), from the late 19th to the 21st century. Under the influence of rationalism men abandoned Christian ethics, jettisoned biblical limits on the authority of civil government, and sought to create rationalistically conceived plans for perfecting man and society through the power of civil government. Under the influence of empiricism men scrapped the limits which Christian ethics and the Constitution place on civil government and sought to remake society and economic life by the application of "science" to the policies of civil government. Under the influence of irrationalism men have sought to have civil government follow the unrestrained will of the president, unelected federal judges, congressional majorities, or a self-anointed intellectual elite. Various strains of socialism (rationalistic utopian socialism in the 19th century, rationalistic democratic socialism in the 19th and 20h centuries, pseudo-scientific Marxian socialism and communism in the 19th and into the 21st centuries, and irrational "pragmatism" and fascism in the 20th and 21st centuries) accompanied these main currents of modern man-centered thought. Together they transformed American liberalism from a small government to big government ideology, radically altered the ethical and political content of American education, used the "public schools" to secularize, indoctrinate and manipulate Americans' thinking, and prepared the populace to look for social and economic "salvation" through an all-powerful, unlimited central government.

Political opportunism has played a large role in the abandonment of our Christian tradition of civil government and law, the circumvention of our Constitution's limitations on civil government authority, the usurpation of power from the state governments, the centralization of power in our national government and its institutions, and the growth of our current gigantic, unlimited, arbitrary, bureaucratic government. Political opportunism has been able to appeal to the sinful desires of many people, rich, poor, and middle class, to live at the expense of others by engaging in legalized theft. The disappointing story of opportunistic use of crises to abandon our

Christian heritage of limited civil government must begin at least with Lincoln's "presidential dictatorship" and the Radical Republicans' congressional tyranny during the War Between the States and Reconstruction; resume with Woodrow Wilson's and the so-called Progressives and their use of the First World War to augment the power of the central government and accustom Americans to socialistic direction of our economic life; and continue with Franklin D. Roosevelt and his Democratic Congress and their use of the Great Depression and World War II to further augment the power of our national government and establish socialistic programs which are still with us.[2]

Lyndon Johnson, using the crisis of the assassination of President Kennedy and the Democrats' landslide victory in 1964, expanded the socialistic "welfare state" established by the "New Deal" with his "Great Society" programsand abandoned the last of the biblical criteria by which previous genuinely charitable efforts had been based. With the exception of a slight slowdown during the Reagan years, post "New Deal" administrations, Republican and Democrat (though the former moving at slower speeds), shaped by the predominant humanistic climate of opinion and often moved by "liberal" crusades, have continued the downward course away from God, God's law, limited government, biblical justice, and liberty and toward the arbitrary will of man, unlimited government, perverted justice, and tyranny.

Christians have done little to alter the course, much less to turn our "ship of state" back to God, righteousness, justice, and liberty.

The political and legal thinking of early Americans at the time of the "founding" of the Republic was dominated by Christianity. The church then taught (as it had done in colonial times) about civil government and law. It spoke—and spoke publicly, via public political sermons delivered on official civil government occasions—to the ethical, political, and historical issues of the day. And it spoke upon the basis of the Bible and Christian theories of "natural law" that were dependent on the Bible for directional light.

By 1853 when the Rev. Mr. Willson published this work Christians had largely ceased to be salt and light to American society, for they had abandoned the Bible as the only authoritative rule of faith and practice for all areas of life—including civil government and law. Despite the fact that civil government is a ministry of God, they had lost interest in it, as Willson rightly complains. Revivalism had led many to believe that all that is needed to heal society is the salvation of individual souls. There was little or no instruction in the whole counsel of God and the application of God's word and law to all areas of thought and life. Emotionalism had led many to reduce Christianity to a series of "experiences" and away from the study of the Bible to deduce doctrines by which to live. Emotionalism had also fueled anti-intellectualism and thereby discouraged the searching of the Scriptures for the answers to the issues of life and politics. Claims of special extra-biblical revelations had undermined the authority of the Scriptures and exalted the pseudo-authority of charismatic leaders. Meanwhile, pietism reduced Christianity to an inward, highly personal thing. Christianity had always been that, but under the influence of the whole Bible it had been a view of the world that is also supposed to influence every area of life. Pietism claimed that civil government and public affairs are outside the realm of the true Christian's concern and led Christians to retreat from political involvement. Also during these years some Christians began to shift from a victorious to a defeatist eschatology which, contrary to the implied promise of Christ in the Great Commission (and contrary to the view of the author of this book), denied the eventual worldwide triumph of Christianity, the Christianization of the nations, and presented evil as triumphing until the return of Christ. The result of such influences was to turn Christians' thinking from the Bible's teachings on civil government and law to that of a man-centered worldview.

Many Christians' abandonment of the biblical teaching that all aspects of man's mind have been damaged by Original Sin—his reason, understanding, and will; his heart, the very core of his being and determiner of his thinking—made them susceptible to man-centered rationalism and empiricism (exclusive faith in the scientific method). Christians' acceptance of Christian theories of "natural law"—forgetting that man's nature is fallen in sinful rebellion against God and God's law, that the whole creation, "nature" itself, is fallen as a result of God's judgment on man's sin, and that the Bible itself presents Scripture as a higher, better ethical standard than "nature"—made them more susceptible to the blandishments of rationalism and scientism, and turned them from the infallibly, fully inspired Bible to the fallen mind of man as their standard for thinking about civil government and law. Rationalism and scientism claimed cures for "social ills." Rationalistic "reformers," as even Ralph Waldo Emerson (1803–1882) noted, virtually all conceived plans—most of them socialistic—for redoing society. Followers of Karl Marx and Friedrich Engels (communists) claimed "science" as the basis for their totalitarian panacea. Abolitionists (as distinct from anti-slavery men) rationalistically sought to end slavery immediately, and violently if necessary, without considering the consequences for all Americans, the people of the South, or even the slaves themselves. Unitarian socialists advocated "free public education" as the cure for all manner of ills, as well as a means of removing the influence of Christianity on society.[3] Advocates of such "reforms," implicitly rejecting a biblical view of civil government, man, and law, turned to the power of civil government to effect the changes they sought. Many Christians fell for some of these "reforms." Many abandoned Christian education for "free public education," and in doing so surrendered parents' authority over the education of their children to the State, its increasingly de-Christianized textbooks, and its rationalistic teachers.

Our time is scientifically, technologically, and economically superior to Willson's but spiritually, morally, and politically inferior to the America and world of his day. We live in an age in which the long growth of unbelief and the failures of the church have compounded Christians' ignorance of the Bible's indispensable teaching on the origin, nature, and purposes of civil government and multiplied the problems which face Christians and their seed.

We need James M. Willson's careful exposition of Romans 13:1–7 which connects the passage with the cardinal governmental principles of Holy Scripture. For his work gave the church in 1853 and gives the church today the scriptural knowledge—the biblical vision—that it needs to understand why we are in the dire situation that we are in; to understand the true nature and purposes of civil government and what sinful, crafty men have done to pervert those purposes. Civil government is not a mere humanly-conceived institution but one ordained by God. It is to be evaluated chiefly by the standard of the word of God revealed in the Scriptures, "in each Testament, and in every form of instruction", not merely by "the light of nature," for that is now too weak in man.

Civil government's purpose is not to satisfy the desires of men—be they rulers or "the people"—but to serve God. The purposes for which civil government exists, Willson rightly notes, are more important than civil government itself, and much more important than the particular form of civil government or the possession of governmental power by any human being(s). These purposes Willson defines from each verse, paying careful attention to the Apostle Paul's wording and reasoning. The rulers of civil government are not a terror to good works, but to the evil. They are to protect those who do "good" and give them praise. Such a claim assumes that there is a way to discern "good" behavior from "evil" behavior. They are to wield "the power of the sword" to punish, and therefore restrain, those who do evil. Paul means by "good" ("good works") and "evil" ("evil works") what the Bible and not any lesser standard defines as good and evil.

The author notes that it is "a most serious error" "that God has ordained any institution among men, or sanctions any, in which the promotion of His glory as the Supreme Law-giver, and the alone object of worship and religious homage, is not a *chief* end". This points clearly to why Christians—and Christian ministers!—should be interested in, study, and teach about civil government. It also highlights another important point made by the author and denied by too many Christians: the "good works" and "evil works" to which Paul refers have to do with "outward acts" prohibited by *both tables of God's law.* The apostle's reasoning leaves no room for justifying the omission of the First Table (laws concerning man's relationship to God) and including only laws based on the Second Table (laws concerning man's relationship to man). Besides, if we omit the First Table of God's law we undermine the authority of the Second Table of the law. If there is no God, there are no rights.

The Declaration of Independence makes this abundantly clear when it states that our "rights" are an endowment from "our Creator." In a world without God, there is no murder or theft.

We need to study books like *The Establishment and Limits of Civil Government* and the Book of Books upon which it is based to retake Christ's ministry of civil government for His glory and to put it to work for our own and our neighbors' good.

That civil government is an institution ordained by God to serve His ethical purposes is sufficient scriptural warrant for the church's interest in the ministry of civil government and sufficient reason to scrap the unbiblical and often inane excuses which Christians have given for evading their responsibility to study, teach about, and become involved in the ministry of civil government.

The God-ordained nature of the institution of civil government requires us to be obedient to it, but the God-ordained purposes of civil government do not require our obedience to the ungodly commands, laws, or regulations of evil, much less tyrannical civil magistrates who occupy positions of authority in the institution of civil government. The Rev. Willson's careful reading of the passage rescues us from false interpretations of the text by Christians and non-Christians: (1) of those who say that it teaches unresisting, unquestioning obedience to civil government officials no matter how ungodly or tyrannical they are; (2) of those who advocate merely passive obedience and non-resistance to unjust laws and tyrannical regimes; (3) of advocates of monarchial absolutism and the divine right of kings—today's equivalent being executive, legislative, and/or judicial absolutism and the "divine right" of the majority; and (4) secularist political thinkers who, seizing upon the misinterpretations of the above schools of thought, seek to portray the Bible as opposed to liberty. These errors are usually avoided, he notes, by dealing with the passage as a whole and not separating the first and second verses from their context. These false interpretations are still with us, doing their damage to truth and liberty. It is not surprising that anti-Christians would distort the teaching of the text, but it is amazing that Christian expositors who (quite rightly) have no trouble deducing the doctrine of the Trinity from Scripture are unable to comprehend that this passage does not teach that we must, not only for fear of the power of the sword used against us but also for a mature conscience's sake, obey every ungodly command or law of wicked rulers. Perhaps if they included verses 8–10—which point directly to God's law—in their study they could see that their "absolute obedience" position requires us to violate our consciences by violating God's laws in order to obey civil government officials' wicked laws and decrees! We are protected against such absurdities—and God's wisdom, goodness and honor are upheld—by the Rev. Willson's careful reading of the text and his refutations of these popular errors.

Beyond this, the apostle's teaching, with that of the Scriptures in other places, implies (1) the right and duty of individual resistance against unjust laws and tyranny; (2) the right and duty of forcible resistance of unjust and tyrannical civil government officials, including the removal of such rulers from office and/or changing the form of civil government; and (3) the right and duty of resistance against foreign or domestic tyranny.

Other significant inferences which the author draws from this and related passages in Scripture are: that civil rulers should be God-fearing men; that civil government is instituted for the promotion of moral as well as social order among men; that civil rulers, "in their official character," are imperatively obliged "to recognize the divine supremacy"; that civil government should extend its protection to every class of people, and especially to the weaker; and that many of the existing governments of the world "have no claim to conscientious acknowledgement". Christians need to ponder these conclusions too.

The church today is like the church of Willson's day, but more so. The vast majority of it has not enough biblical sense to keep its children out of the government schools—which are much farther advanced in unbelief, in hostility to Christianity, in the volume and seriousness of lies which they convey to their pupils, and in their techniques for behavioral manipulation of young minds than were the "public schools" of a century and a half ago. Thus they allow their children to be indoctrinated with the false doctrines of secular humanism, the established religion of the government schools; to have their morals perverted; and to have them programmed with the lies which compose the social, economic, and political agenda of the leftists who control the "public schools." Many think themselves too holy to study civil government and politics, much less get involved in the two. Many deny that it is a legitimate duty of the church to study, preach, and teach about civil government and law—much less for Christians to devote their time, talents, resources, and energy to politics. Many would rather "play at church" than seek to protect the church—and our non-Christian neighbors—from "the power of the sword" in the wicked hands of the enemies of God who now dominate our civil governments. Rather than instruct their people in the Bible's teachings about civil government, law, public life, the issues of the day,[4] the duties of civil magistrates, the duties of citizens, and the principles of obedience and resistance to civil rule, they preoccupy their minds with the events of the worship service, the excitement of the congregation, ecclesiastical issues, or preaching what most people want to hear. If they do minister by evangelizing men (and bless them if they do!), they do not instruct men in the things of the ministry of civil government. They do nothing to get Christians to influence, much less govern, God's ministry of civil government. No wonder there are no public political sermons preached on official civil government occasions today!

Most church leaders today surrender the ministry of civil government to the enemies of God. They do nothing to defend God's people or anyone else against the schemes and actions of evil men who claim absolute, arbitrary power for civil government, the authority to interfere in all areas of our lives, the authority to subject us to the rule of global governments, the authority to stifle what liberty remains to us, the authority to persecute Christians and opponents of the current regime; and, via government-controlled medical care, the authority to withhold medical care from many of us and our fellow citizens. Many Christians see the frightening trends but continue to interpret them as portending the imminent return of Christ (as some of them have done for more than fifty years); meanwhile, they violate His commandment to us to occupy until He returns (Luke 19:13), doing nothing to influence Christ's ministry of civil government for His glory, and nothing to assure that civil government, by applying God's law, fulfills the law of love, "love works no evil to his neighbor" (Romans 13:10).

The church today *needs* books like the Rev. Willson's careful exposition of this crucial New Testament passage. It needs to read them, to study them, to measure them by the Scriptures, and to apply their sound teachings to influence God's ministry of civil government for His glory, the protection of His people, the good of our neighbors, and, as much as God's law will allow, the good of mankind.

NOTES

1. Benjamin F. Morris, *The Christian Life and Character of the Civil Institutions of the United States* (Powder Springs, Georgia: American Vision, [1864] 2007); William J. Federer, *America's God and Country Encyclopedia of Quotations* (Coppell, Texas: FAME Publishing, Inc., 1994); Ellis Sandoz, *A Government of Laws: Political Theory, Religion, and the American Founding* (Baton Rouge and London: Louisiana State University Press, 1990); Charles S. Hyneman and Donald S. Lutz, eds., *American Political Writing during the Founding Era 1760-1805*, 2 volumes (Indianapolis: Liberty Press, 1983); M. Stanton Evans, *The Theme Is Freedom; Religion, Politics, and the American Tradition* (Washington, D.C.: Regnery, 1994); John Eidsmoe, *Christianity and the Constitution: The Faith of Our Founding Fathers* (Grand Rapids: Baker Book House, 1987); Gary DeMar, *America's Christian History* (Powder Springs, Georgia: American Vision, 2005); David J. Brewer, *The United States: A Christian Nation* (Powder Springs, Georgia: American Vision, [1905] 1996); Bishop Charles B. Galloway, *Christianity and the American Commonwealth; or The Influence of Christianity in Making This Nation* (Powder Springs, Georgia: American Vision, [1898] 2005); Rousas J. Rushdoony, *This Independent Republic; Studies in the Nature and Meaning of American History* (Vallecito, California: Chalcedon Foundation, [1964] 2008); Rousas J. Rushdoony, *The Nature of the American System* (Vallecito, California: Chalcedon Foundation, [1965] 2008); and Archie P. Jones, "Christianity in the Constitution: The Intended Meaning of the Religion Clauses of the First Amendment," unpublished PhD. Dissertation, University of Dallas, 1991.

2. Robert Higgs, *Crisis and Leviathan; Critical Episodes in the Growth of American Government* (New York: Oxford University Press, 1987).

3. Samuel L. Blumenfeld, *Is Public Education Necessary?* (Boise, Idaho: The Paradigm Co., 1985).

4. Gary DeMar, ed., *Passing the Torch of Liberty to a New Generation* (Powder Springs, GA: American Vision, 2009) and Ellis Sandoz, ed., *Political Sermons of the American Founding Era, 1730–1805*, 2 vols. (Indianapolis: Liberty Fund, 1998).

PREFACE

The subject of civil government is, in all its aspects, of no little importance. It occupies a large share of men's thoughts in all enlightened countries, and awakens, just now, the liveliest concern. This is not strange; for its influence is felt in every department of human action. It has to do with the peace, the order, the material prosperity of the commonwealth; with the rights and liberties of the citizens, and exercises no inconsiderable influence upon the interests of morals and religion. In all these respects, in the last particularly, the institution of civil government is deserving the attention of the Christian and of the Christian minister. Moreover, the inspired writers take occasion, not infrequently, to state, sometimes summarily in the doctrinal form, and sometimes in narrative and in detail, leading principles by which the intelligent and faithful may be directed as to the part which they are to take in setting up, in administering, or in supporting political constitutions. Hence, no apology is necessary in entering upon such an examination as that which is now proposed. The topic itself is of great moment, and the light and authority of God's Word are before us.

Again: these researches are imperatively called for, inasmuch as the particular passage to which the attention of the reader is asked—Romans 13:1–7—has been grievously perverted. One class of expositors endeavor to derive from these teachings of Paul the offensive principle of unresisting, unquestioning subjection to civil authority of whatever stamp. Rulers, say they, may be ungodly, tyrannical, immoral—they may subvert the liberties, and take away the rights of their subjects. Still, but one course is open; even to such rulers and to such authority, there must be yielded at least a "passive obedience;" no "resis-

"I always admired virtue—but I could never imitate it."

KING CHARLES II

"I shall make it my endeavour to preserve the government in Church and State as it is by law established."

KING JAMES II

tance" is ever lawful, though made by the entire body of the oppressed, and that under peril of eternal damnation: for "the powers that be are ordained of God; and he that resisteth the power receiveth unto himself damnation."

This principle was a very prominent topic among the controversies that arose in England after the restoration of Charles II, in 1660. The advocates of high Episcopacy—particularly the Oxford theologians—stated it in the strongest terms, maintaining the divine right of the restored government to an unlimited allegiance. It was revived, after the Revolution of 1688, by the non-jurors and their friends, who urged it against that settlement of affairs. The conflict raged long and was very bitter; for all, whether in church or state, who favored the expulsion of James II, and the establishment of the succession to the throne in the house of Brunswick,—

"The design of the Reformation, was to restore Christianity to what it was at first, and to purge it of those Corruptions, with which it was over-run in the later and darker Ages."

GILBERT BURNET
(1643–1715)

the friends of civil liberty,—were equally earnest in maintaining the right of a nation to take measures for the prevention of tyranny and of an arbitrary power over the rights of the subjects.

All these, including such men as Burnet (1643–1715) and Benjamin Hoadly (1676–1761)—while they vindicated monarchy as the best form of government, in this agreeing with their opponents, were no less vehement in asserting and also in proving that the apostle's doctrine implied certain limitations; that it must be interpreted so as not to conflict with the plain dictates of reason, or the liberties of nations. This form of the controversy regarding this celebrated passage, has passed away. Even Oxford found it impossible to carry out its own doctrine; and hence when James II attempted to lay violent hands upon its chartered rights and immunities, Oxford resisted: it ate its own words, and took rank with the most decided adversaries of that Popish king in his assaults upon English Law and Protestantism. While power was in the hands of a court professedly Protestant, and zealous for the ecclesiastical supremacy of the Church of England, it was all well enough; but when a new government arose which sought to transfer all the posts of honor and influence in church and state into popish hands, these conscientious defenders of an absolute divine right took the alarm, and refused to be bound by their own repeatedly asserted doctrines. After the Revolution, this principle did not outlast that generation which felt itself chagrined at the toleration of dissenters from the established religion. They had fought at a disadvantage, and lost ground. A new generation arose, and at last, as a topic of controversy, the subject was dropped, and hence, whatever private views may have been since entertained by the more bigoted loyalists and ecclesiastics, it has long ceased to figure in the annals of literature.

However, even the "exploded" doctrine of "non-resistance" has not entirely succumbed. It has found a place in the commentaries of Robert Haldane and Thomas Chalmers, and still lingers in some minds; at least, in the form of doubts as to the propriety and lawfulness of setting aside institutions and men—by violence, if necessary,—that have proved themselves incompetent to answer the ends of political arrangements and authority.

"We have no faith in the efficacy of mechanic's institutes, or even of primary and elementary schools, for building up a virtuous and well conditioned peasantry, so long as they stand dissevered from the lessons of Christian piety."

THOMAS CHALMERS
(1780–1847)

There is another class of expositors, embracing a large proportion of the more modern, and some of the ancient, commentators; who, while they admit that while nations may remodel their constitutions so as to suit themselves, and even resort to violence for the overthrow of tyrannical power—in other words, they admit the right of revolution—still hold and teach, as the doctrine of this passage, that so long as a government exists, whatever be its character, it is entitled to, and may demand, in the name of God, a conscientious obedience to its laws, unless they conflict with the laws of God.

This is a view highly plausible and popular, and yet to say nothing, at present, of its inconsistency, (for, how could there be a revolutionary movement, unless conscience had previously ceased to feel any obligation to respect and honor and fear the existing government?) it will appear in the sequel that it gains no countenance from the teachings of Paul, and for the reason that the passage makes no reference, as we think will appear upon strict examination of its terms, to any "power" but that which answers in some good measure the ends of its insti-

"All that we can possibly collect from his (Paul's), injunctions in this place is this, that it is the indispensable duty of subjects to submit themselves to such governors as answer the good ends of their institution."

BENJAMIN HOADLY

tution. Whatever may be the regard, if any, due to an immoral and tyrannical, and, of course, hurtful government, this passage makes no reference to it. It teaches one set of truths, and one only,—the nature, functions, and claims of a good government. In the language of Bishop Benjamin Hoadly:

> As the apostle's words stand at present, and have ever stood, it is impossible to prove that he had in view any particular magistrate acting against the ends of his institution....

and again,

All that we can possibly collect from his (Paul's), injunctions in this place is this, that it is the indispensable duty of subjects to submit themselves to such governors as answer the good ends of their institution. There is nothing to make it probable that Paul had any governors particularly in his eye, who were a terror to good works and not to evil, or that he had any other design in this place but to press submission to magistrates, upon those who acknowledged none to be due in point of conscience, from the end of their institution, and the usefulness of their office. And in whatever instances submission can be proved to be due from this argument, I am ready to acknowledge that Paul extended it to all such instances. But as for submission in other instances, the apostle's reasoning here cannot defend or justify it, but rather implies the contrary. For if submission be a duty because magistrates are carrying forward a good work, the peace and happiness of human society, which is the argument Paul useth, it is implied in this that resistance is rather a duty than submission, when they manifestly destroy the public peace and happiness.[1]

We are aware that the truth of these assertions remains to be proved: their truth will appear in the analysis of the passage, but we would now state it distinctly and emphatically, for it is the key to the right understanding of this, and parallel passages. Keeping this in mind, the scope and bearing of Paul's doctrine on civil government and submission of authority, is as clear as a sunbeam. He gives no countenance to any slavish doctrine— to any claim of divine right to do wrong—to any principle that would tie up our hands, or in the least interfere with the right of the Christian citizen to "prove," by moral and scripture rules, as

---

1. Hoadly's *Submission To the Powers That Be*; pages 49, 22, 50.

well as by the laws of self-preservation, any and all institutions and laws. In what light we are to regard tyrannical and ungodly powers, we may ascertain elsewhere, but cannot here, except, and the exception is important, that inasmuch as Paul gives us the character of government, *as God approves it*, and then enjoins subjection, we can pretty directly infer that in case a government does not possess, at least, a due measure of the requisite qualifications, the command to obey cannot apply to it.

A greater interest is, moreover, to be attached to such investigations as we propose, from the fact that infidels of our times make use of this passage to serve their own purposes. We live in an age and country of liberal ideas regarding government—an age when the rights of the people are watched with the utmost sagacity and vigilance. Popular rights are matters taken for granted, and anything that runs counter to them is at once rejected. Infidelity attempts to turn this feeling in behalf of liberty into its own channel—to rouse it against the Bible, as if it favored absolute and irresponsible power; and they avail themselves, and with no little success, of the mistaken exposition of the very passage before us. The expositors to whom we have referred intend to strengthen the arm of any and all civil authority—these interpretations the infidel school use for the overthrow of the authority of the Bible. Both are met and foiled by one process—simply by a just analysis of the passage itself.

This we now proceed to attempt, hoping to demonstrate, on the one hand, that a good government finds here both a guide and a pillar—and on the other, that a bad government finds not the faintest shadow of countenance, but is inferentially, but not the less effectually, condemned.

1

Exposition of Romans 13:1-7

Let every soul be subject unto the higher powers. For there is no power but of God: the powers that be are ordained of God. Whosoever therefore resisteth the power, resisteth the ordinance of God: and they that resist shall receive to themselves damnation. For rulers are not a terror to good works, but to the evil. Wilt thou then not be afraid of the power? do that which is good, and thou shalt have praise of the same: For he is the minister of God to thee for good. But if thou do that which is evil, be afraid; for he beareth not the sword in vain: for he is the minister of God, a revenger to execute wrath upon him that doeth evil. Wherefore ye must needs be subject, not only for wrath, but also for conscience sake. For for this cause pay ye tribute also: for they are God's ministers, attending continually upon this very thing. Render therefore to all their dues: tribute to whom tribute is due; custom to whom custom; fear to whom fear; honour to whom honour.

This passage will be found, upon careful analysis, to embrace the following topics:

I. The duty in general of obedience to civil authority: v. 1.

II. General considerations enforcing this obedience: v. 1 and 2.

III. The design of the appointment of rulers, or of the institution of government: v. 3.

IV. The application of these principles to the case of both good and bad citizens: v. 3, 4.

V. The principle of obedience to civil rule: v. 5.

VI. A more specific statement of the duties owing to civil government, as previously described; v. 6, 7.

SECTION I

The duty, in general, of obedience to civil authority.

"Let every soul be subject to the higher powers" (Verse 1).

1. *Civil governments are called "Powers."* The term here used (εξουσια) is employed to denote any species of authority—paternal, ecclesiastical, magisterial. That in this instance it means civil rule, is abundantly clear from the whole tenor of the passage. It is important, however, to remark that it designates civil government, not as an institution endued with ability to execute its will—for this another term (δυναμις) would have been more appropriate—but as invested with the right to enact and administer law. "By what authority," (εξουσια) say the scribes to our Lord, "doest thou these things?"—"who hath given thee this authority?" (Matthew 21:23)[1]

2. *They are called "Higher Powers."* The word (υπερεχου-σαις) here rendered "higher," properly signifies prominence, or eminence, and hence it comes to mean "excellent," or "excelling," and must be translated by these or equivalent expressions in a number of passages in the New Testament. "Let each esteem other better (υπερεχοντας) than themselves" (Philippians 2:3). "And the peace of God, which passeth (υπερεχουσα)

---

1. See Appendix A, p. 133.

all understanding (Philippians 4:7). "For the excellency (δια το υπερεχον) of the knowledge of Christ Jesus my Lord" (Philippians 3:8). In fact, the passage now before us, and 1 Peter 2:13, a parallel passage, are the only instances in which our translators have furnished a different rendering. Hence, some expositors have been disposed to lay no little stress upon this epithet, as distinctly defining the character of the powers here intended, and as limiting to such the subjection here enjoined, the "excelling powers;" that is, powers possessing a due measure of the qualifications requisite to the rightful exercise of the power of civil rule.

THE APOSTLE PAUL

That such is the fact—that the duty of subjection to civil rule is not absolutely unlimited—that it must be determined by other and higher considerations than the *mere* fact that it exists and brandishes "the sword," is a most important truth— a truth nowhere taught more clearly, as we shall find, than in the passage before us. Still we are not disposed to insist upon any different rendering. We neither deny nor affirm. To elicit the true meaning and import of the passage does not require the aid of minute, and, after all, doubtful criticism.[2] Civil rule is a "higher" power—it is vested with an eminent dignity. It spreads its aegis—when properly constituted and administered—over the whole commonwealth, with all its varied interests, and claims an unopposed supremacy. There is an inherent majesty in lawful governmental power calculated and designed to impress subjects and citizens of every class and character with a salutary awe. And whether the attributes of inherent moral excellency be expressed in the designation here given or not, it may be readily inferred, for "power," without moral character, is a monster indeed.

It is, however, government and not the particular magistrates by whom authority is exercised, to which Paul here refers. The distinction is important. "Rulers" are mentioned for the first time in verse 3. He now treats of the institution of civil rule. The "powers"—the "higher" powers,—Government in the abstract—the *institution* of civil rule.

3. *Subjection is enjoined to civil government*; verse 1: "Be subject:" that is, voluntarily, freely, and cheerfully rendering allegiance and homage, and yielding a uniform and conscientious obedience to the wholesome laws enacted by the "higher powers." In other words, what is here meant is something far different from an unresisting submission to what cannot

---

2. See Appendix B, p. 135.

be helped, as when the unarmed traveler submits to be despoiled by the highway robber. This kind of submission is, indeed, often called for. The slave must, of necessity, do the bidding of his master. The power is unjust. It may be tyrannically exercised. It is, in its very nature, despotic. But the victim of wrong has, for the time, no alternative. By obedience alone can he secure exemption from greater suffering. So the unhappy subject of arbitrary civil rule. He is beneath the iron heel of the despot. He must obey. But it is a forced obedience, wrung from him by the irresistible might of the tyrant's scepter. So, also, the Christian may be compelled to yield a kind of submission to overwhelming power. He is in its hand. The sword is ready to enforce the mandates of unholy authority. The slave, and the subject of despotic civil rule, alike submit; but both for the same reason—the impossibility of escape, or of successful resistance.

To nothing of all this does the inspired apostle here refer. He employs a term (υποτασσεσθω) that denotes an orderly and due submission—a genuine and hearty subjection; and to fix the meaning of the injunction beyond dispute, he defines it more fully, afterwards, in verses 5 and 7: "Wherefore ye must needs be subject, not only for wrath, but also for conscience sake: fear to whom fear—honor to whom honor." In short, whatever may be the duty of the oppressed, and whatever his rights, Paul does not here consider either. He deals with but one topic: the duty of subjection to civil government—civil government as he afterwards describes it, with its duties, its character and its claims. To such a government there is due, not mere obedience, but an obedience hearty and prompt; an obedience importing an acknowledgment of its being and authority—an obedience originating in an intelligent perception and appreciation of its character, design, and happy fruits. But even this, we may safely say, is not inconsiderate

13

or unlimited, for it is an obedience limited, after all, by the paramount claims of the law of God. For surely none but an atheist can deliberately affirm that even the law of the land can set aside, weaken or nullify the authority of the law of God. To the *best* government, obedience can be yielded only in things lawful; for there is a "higher law" to which rulers and subjects are alike amenable. "The heavens do rule." There is a God above us, and "to Him every knee shall bow, and every tongue shall confess that Jesus Christ

Daniel Before Nebuchadnezzar

is Lord, to the glory of God the Father" (Philippians 2:10,11). And, surely, if obedience to the best government is thus limited, it need hardly be added, that submission to an unholy power does not go beyond this. This also is limited by the law of God. It can only be yielded when this can be done without sin. In every other case, the subject—the slave even—should imitate the noble example of Daniel, and of myriads of the faithful before and since, and suffer rather than sin.

To return: the duty here inculcated is that of a hearty recognition of a rightful civil authority, together with an active support of its claims, and a personal and respectful obedience to its lawful enactments.

4. *This injunction lies upon every citizen.* "Let every soul be subject," etc.[3] (v. 1) There is no exception. The rich and the poor, the young and the old, the Christian and the infidel, the minister of Christ as well as the private member of the church must be subject. In this lies much of the emphasis of the apostle's language; for it is clearly intended to rebuke the notion, early entertained, and that has still found a place among the professed followers of Christ, that it is unworthy of a Christian to be subject to civil rule; that having one master, even Christ, obedience is due, in no sense, not even with suitable limitations, to any other authority; and, also, to confute, beforehand, the arrogance of the popish priesthood, who claim, as all know, exemption from civil control. Equally opposed to both these is the explicit declaration of Paul, "Let *every soul* be subject to the higher powers."

Nor can this be wrested to the establishment of any authority on the part of the civil magistrate over the church of

---

3. We might, perhaps, have adduced this clause—the term "soul" particularly—as an argument confirming our interpretation of the command, "be subject." It is not outward submission merely, but a subjection in which the "soul" goes along with the external act.

Christ. The church is an independent society. Her constitution, her doctrines, her laws, her administration, all are from Christ. To him alone is she subject. She exists, indeed, among and in the kingdoms of the world, but owes no allegiance to any other Head than to Christ. To claim supremacy over her is a presumptuous and unwarranted usurpation; God alone is Lord of the conscience.

INFERENCES

1. Christians should endeavor to understand, and should take suitable interest in the subject of civil government. It is neither remote from them, nor too unholy to occupy their attention. From the mere contests of faction they may, indeed, stand aloof; but surely, that which attracted the attention of an inspired apostle is not beneath the study of the most spiritually minded of the followers of Christ. They should study the subject, moreover; for without this, they cannot with becoming high intelligence perform their own duty respecting it.

2. The Christian minister may and ought to present the doctrine of the word of God, on this, as on other subjects of which the inspired writers treat. The time was, when it would have been necessary to argue elaborately in defense of this statement. It is not necessary now. The pulpit has been compelled to enter this field—long almost abandoned. An age of, at least, attempted social reformation, has driven every party in turn to seek the powerful aid of the Christian ministry, and while we cannot in many instances find much to commend in the manner in which the subject has been presented, it is still so far well, that portions of the word of God which exhibit the character, functions, and claims of civil power, are no longer regarded as forbidden ground. Still, there is need of wisdom. In such discussions, the ambassador of Christ should

keep close to the footsteps of his Master and of his inspired followers, and rising above the transient conflicts and unworthy behests of party, should essay to exhibit and illustrate the entire subject of governmental arrangements and polity, in a manner becoming an exalted moral institution—so as to bring a revenue of glory to Christ the Supreme Lawgiver.

2

Enforcing the Duty of Obedience to Civil Rule

> For there is no power but of God: the powers that be are ordained of God. Whosoever therefore resisteth the power, resisteth the ordinance of God: and they that resist shall receive to themselves damnation. (Verses 1 and 2).

Having stated the duty, the apostle now proceeds to show the grounds on which it rests, insisting upon two classes of arguments, and:

1. *They derive their power from God*, or in other words, government is a divine institution, originating in, and of course, sanctioned by the will of God.

For (1.) *"There is no power but of God."* This is true, whatever sense we attach to the word "power." All physical power—all executive energy, in every department of creation, is from God. "In Him we live, and move, and have our being" (Acts 17:28). In this sense the power of evil beasts and even of the devil, is from God. "By Him all things consist" (Colossians 1:17). Again, if we understand by "power," the possession of the reins of government, it is, certainly, through Him that kings are permitted to occupy their thrones and that, whatever the steps by which they may have succeeded to the seat of authority. Pharaoh was "raised up" in the course of that providence which controls all the affairs of men. God "gave the kingdom" to Jeroboam. The same hand "raised up" Cyrus, and our Lord expressly declares to Pilate, the unholy Roman governor,

> Thou couldest have no power at all against me, except it were given to thee from above (John 19:11).

CHRIST BEFORE PONTIUS PILATE

Even the devil has "power," in this sense, from God. Does Paul mean no more than this? Assuredly he means something far different. This clause assigns a reason for that hearty subjection which the apostle had just enjoined. But, surely, the mere fact that one possesses "power," can be no reason why his claims should be acknowledged, and his laws conscientiously obeyed. If so, the slave—ay, the slave who has been stolen from his own land and ignominiously held as a chattel—would be required to admit, as from God, the validity of his master's claims. To throw off his chains, and make his way to his native home as a freeman, would be rebellion against God. No doctrine could be more agreeable than this to tyrants, and to all that panders to unholy power; for, if this be Paul's meaning, there is no despot, no usurper, no bloody conqueror, but could plead the divine sanction and, more than this, the devil himself could lay the teachings of Paul under contribution to enforce his pre-eminently unholy authority. An interpretation which leads to such monstrous conclusions—that would bind the nations to the footstool of power with iron chains, and utterly crush every free aspiration—that would invest with the sanctions of the divine name the most flagrant usurpation and the most unrelenting despotism—stands self-condemned.

But we go further. Providence is not a rule of action. Sin and evil of all kinds exist in the course of the same providential administration, as that which furnishes a place for governments which contemn God and oppress mankind. And yet who claims for sin a divine *sanction*? Who denies to the suffering the right to rid themselves of their trials? Carry out this interpretation, and you furnish the bloody government of the Papal States an impregnable defense against the efforts of the liberators of Italy.

The truth is, the apostle has no reference here at all to anything but the *institution* of government;[1] and designs to assert, and does assert, that there is no authority properly exercised over men, but that which God has established. This is true in the largest sense: for man is God's creature and subject, and he who sets up claims to dominion over him must be prepared to show that he exercises an authority of that sort and of that character which bears the stamp and sanction of divine institution. Had Paul, indeed, said no more, it might have been argued, with great plausibility, that he designed in this passage to give tyrants of the earth, what they have always claimed, the sanction of the Most High in their course of monstrous iniquity. Even then, however, we would have endeavored, and we think successfully, to vindicate the word of God against so abhorrent a conclusion. But Paul did not stop with these general assertions. He proceeds, as will presently appear, to define, with great distinctness and brevity, his own meaning: to designate the sort of "power" to which he alludes: not any and *every* existing government, but that which answers the end of its institution. In short, the design of this clause: "There is no power but of God," is merely to assert the general principle that subjection is due to civil government, inasmuch as government is a divine institution. This appears more distinctly from what follows.

2. *"The powers that be are ordained of God."* The prime fallacy of many commentaries on this entire passage consists in taking for granted that this phrase—this celebrated phrase—"the powers that be"—means all and any existing governments. This cannot be. The considerations already advanced, in set-

---

1. *"Power* is to be distinguished from *persons*; for Paul loved polity and power; but Caligula and Nero he execrated as monsters in nature, instruments of the devil, and pests of the human race." (*Lectures on Romans* by Andrew Melville, Edin., 1850, p. 487).

ting aside a similar interpretation of the preceding clause, forbid it. Nor are there wanting others, equally conclusive. Of Israel it is said, referring to the establishment of an independent government by the ten tribes under Jeroboam, "They have set up kings, but not by me; they have made princes, and I knew (approved) it not" (Hosea 8:4). And the prophet Daniel, and afterwards the apostle John, expressly and frequently denominate the Roman Empire a "beast."

The former, a

> beast, dreadful and terrible, and strong exceedingly; and it had great iron teeth: it devoured and brake in pieces, and stamped the residue with the feet of it (Daniel 7:11).

DANIEL'S DREAM OF THE FOUR BEASTS

The latter, a

> beast having seven heads and ten horns, and on
> it horns ten crowns, and on its heads the name of
> blasphemy (Revelation 17:1).

THE SEVEN-HEADED BEAST OF REVELATION

Surely such a description was never given of a government that
could lay any solid claim to be "ordained of God;" at least, in
any other sense than the pestilence is God's ordinance, existing in his providence, but to be shunned and banished as soon
as possible.[2] And, in fact, for this end, among others, the gospel

---

2. "So are fevers, plagues, fires, inundations, tempests, and the like. And yet
Almighty God not only permits, but requires us to use all prudent methods of resisting and stopping their fury, but is far from expecting that we should lie down,
and do nothing to save ourselves from perishing in such calamities. So likewise
are robbers and cut-throats God's judgments, but this doth not prove that you
must submit yourselves and families to be ruined at their pleasure. So again are
inferior magistrates, if they make use of their power to fall with violence upon
their neighbors, and attempt their lives, or the ruin of their families; and yet they

is sent into the world. It is the "stone cut out of the mountain without hands," which is to "smite the great image (Daniel 2) and break it in pieces." One ordinance of God, smiting, and breaking in pieces, another! The term "powers" here denote, as before, the institution of civil rule. This, with all other kinds of power that may be lawfully exercised among men, is "ordained of God." In other words, the Most High has made provision for the exercise of civil authority. He has not left mankind to be controlled by no other government than that of parents over their children, of masters over their servants, of church rulers over private Christians. He has, also, provided for the setting up and administering of another kind of power, having its own peculiar ends, its rules, its limits, and its administrators—the power of civil government. God has willed the existence of a national organization and polity; and, in so doing, has fixed its ends, which it must subserve; has given it a supreme law, which it must observe; has bound it by limits which it may not pass over. In short, God has "ordained"[3] civil government as Christ has ordained the ministry of reconciliation, not by merely willing its existence, but by prescribing its duties, its functions, its end, and its limitations.

No other meaning can be affixed of the language of the apostle, consistently with due reverence for Him who is the

---

may be resisted, and their illegal violence repelled by violence. And so, lastly, are foreign enemies and invaders, always reckoned amongst God's judgments, and amongst the most remarkable of them; and yet there is no necessity, I hope, from hence, of tamely submitting ourselves to them: and no argument from hence, against the lawfulness or honorableness of resisting them. Either, therefore, let it be shown, that this objection holds good in other of God's judgments; or, that there is something peculiar in this to exempt it from the common rule; or let it be acknowledged that it signifies nothing in the present case." *Hoadly's Submission To the Powers That Be.* London, 1718, p. 85. Hoadly presents this, it will be seen, as an answer to the objection, that bad governments are to be submitted to, and not thrown off, because they are judgments of God. It comes in as well here.

3. The marginal translation, "ordered," is rather better than that of the text.

Holy One and the Just, the rightful and beneficent moral Governor. Can it be, for a moment, believed, that God has made man a social being—placed him in society, and thus necessitated, by the very laws of the human constitution, the establishment of civil rule, and that he has, after all, set no bounds to the authority, no hedge about the claims of civil rulers? That, after all, He has left this whole matter to be lawfully managed, not by law, even His law, not by rule, but merely according to human caprice, or, what is far worse, human ambition, self-seeking, pride, and violence? And, then, as the issue of the matter, that in case a government exist, whatever the ends it aims at, whatever the principles that guide it administration, whether it be just or unjust, God-fearing or infidel, liberal or despotic, it exists, and He acknowledges it as "ordained" by Him, and as entitled to the regard, homage and obedience of its subjects? This cannot be. God is not so indifferent to His own glory, or to the welfare of man, and particularly of the church. He never intended, we may assert, with entire confidence, to sign, if we may so speak, a blank, and then leave man to fill it up according to his pleasure. Every attribute of God forbids this. Paul teaches no such doctrine.

The terms employed by the apostle, and the connection of the clauses, accord precisely with these views. He first asserts "power is not, except from God:"[4] God alone is the source of legitimate authority. He is sovereign. Man is His. Power, not derived from God, is ever illegitimate. It is mere usurpation; as, for example, the Pope's claim to reign in the church, and over the nations. The apostle then adds, in vindication of civil government, "the powers that be"—governmental institutions; "are arranged under God,"[5] or if this be preferred, "by God." There

---

4. Ου γαρ εστιν εξουσια ειμη απο Θεου.

5. Αι δε ουσαι εξουσιαι, υπο του Θεου τεταγμεναι εισιν. We here quote from the commentary of Andrew Melville. He says, "The third argument is taken

is such a "power" as that of civil rule. It is among the kinds of authority for which the Most High has made provision, and to which he has assigned the requisite laws and functions.

But we rest our interpretation upon no mere verbal criticism. God is the only source of power. And God has in the sense in which we have explained the term, "ordained" civil government. He is the source of power, that power of which Paul speaks, not as he endows with physical strength, or even as He opens the way, in his providence, for its successful employment in subjugating mankind; but as he has authorized the exercise of that particular kind of authority; of course, putting upon it, when measurably conformed to his institution, the impress of his own dignity, and the sanction of his law.[6]

Is it inquired, where this institution is found? The reply has been, in part, anticipated. In the constitution of man, and in the principles of piety, of equity, of beneficence, originally implanted in the human heart, but now, much more clearly, in the written Scriptures, which abound with instruction, addressed to rulers and people, and furnishing all the light mankind need for the organization and administration of the most salutary political regimen. The passage before us is an example. It is

---

from the order divinely constituted under God—for the glory of God; for so I interpret υπο του, etc. Not so much 'from God' which has already been said, as 'powers are arranged under God.' Which with the article τας ουσιας he calls εξουσιας—as if he had said τας ουτως, etc., 'which are truly powers' and deserve the name. Whence, an impious and unjust tyranny, which is not of God, as such, nor accords with the divine order, he excludes, as illegitimate, from this legitimate obedience." Comment. p. 497.

6. "And this may serve to explain yet farther in what sense these higher powers are from God; viz., as they act agreeably to his will, which is, that they should promote the happiness and good of human society, which Paul all along supposes them to do. And consequently, when they do the contrary, they cannot be said to be from God, or to act by his authority, any more than an inferior magistrate may be said to act by a prince's authority, while he acts directly contrary to his will." Hoadly, p. 5.

proper, however, to add, that instruction is given in the word of God, not so much in regard to the particular form which the government should assume, as in reference to the ends it should seek, the principles that should guide the administration, and the character of those into whose hands national affairs should be committed.

This is Paul's first argument enforcing the duty of obedience, and to demonstrate that it is not beneath the dignity of the Christian to be subject to civil government. So far from offending Christ, such subjection honors him—for it is yielded to a divine institution, and for the same reason, it cannot safely be withheld. Hence Paul argues,

2. *From the sin and danger of resisting civil authority, and*

(1.) The sin. "Whosoever, therefore, resisteth the power, resisteth the ordinance of God."—Verse 2nd.

The distinction is still kept up between the institution— "the ordinance" of God, and the magistrate in whose hands the reins of government happen to be found. "Whosoever resisteth the power." A most important distinction. For, in truth, there are occasions when it is not merely lawful, but a matter of high and imperative duty, to resist authority. The case of the high priest, Azariah, and his brethren, who withstood Uzziah, the king of Judah, in his attempt to pass over the limits of his power and obtrude into the priest's office, is well known to every reader of the Bible:

> It pertaineth not unto thee, Uzziah, to burn incense unto the Lord; but to the priests, the sons of Aaron, that are consecrated to burn incense: go out of the sanctuary, for thou hast trespassed (2 Chronicles 26:18).

KING UZZIAH'S SIN

And still more to the purpose are the cases of Shadrach, Meshech, and Abednego, and afterwards Daniel, who all refused compliance with laws enacted by the then supreme authority in Babylon (Daniel 3:6).

SHADRACH, MESHACH, AND ABEDNEGO

To the same effect is the refusal of Peter and John to obey the command of the Jewish magistracy "not to speak at all, nor teach in the name of Jesus."

They reply,

> Whether it be right in the sight of God to hearken unto you more than unto God, judge ye (Acts 4:18, 19).

Indeed, until of late, the duty of refusing to obey the commands of the civil power, when they conflict with duty to God was never, so far as we know, denied by any bearing the name of Christian. It is certain that the advocates of the doctrine of "passive obedience and non-resistance" during the 17th and 18th centuries in England, did not go so far as this. The very terms in which they announced their doctrine make this manifest, "*passive* obedience, *non-resistance.*" They acknowledge a higher law than the enactments of human, and, of course, fallible, and often impious power. The first prominent enun-

Thomas Hobbes of Malmesbury

"I put for the general inclination of all mankind, a perpetual and restless desire of power after power, that ceaseth only in death."

"It is not wisdom but Authority that makes a law."

ciation of the principle of unlimited and unquestioning obedience, was reserved for an atheist—Hobbes of Malmesbury (1588–1679).

Denying the existence of any fixed standard of right—and, consequently, of any such things as virtue and vice—this speculative philosopher resolved all the laws of morality into one—the will of the legislature. But who were his disciples? None but the godless, the dissipated, the scorners of all that is sacred. The heart of England was shocked at the daring attempt to dethrone the Almighty. It was reserved for another age and another land to hear and assent to the blasphemous assertion, that the law of the land overrides all other laws, and *must* be obeyed under penalty of resisting the ordinance of God.

But we may go further, and assert that Paul did not intend, by the language before us, to forbid even the forcible resistance of unjust and tyrannical civil magistrates, not even when that resistance is made with the avowed design of displacing offending rulers, or, it may be, the change of the very form of government itself. There are few in this land, or in any free country, to deny the right of a nation to rid itself of oppressive power—whether foreign or domestic. The right of revolution, for the purpose of throwing off usurping or tyrannical rule, need not, now and here, be defended. That question was settled in England by the Revolution of 1688, when the nation, rising in its might, expelled James II as an enemy to the constitutional rights and liberties of the people.

The separate national and independent existence of these United States is the fruit of successful revolution. And where is the American—the American Christian—who does not rejoice in the hope that the principles of liberty will spread and prevail, even though they be ultimately established upon the wreck of thrones demolished or overturned?

KING JAMES II

"T'was the divine Providence that drove me early out of my native country, and t'was the same providence ordered it so that I past most of the twelve years I was abroad in Catholic kingdoms, by which means I came to know what their religion was."

Does the Spirit of God here condemn these efforts of the nations to rid themselves of the yoke of despots? Does this passage rivet the chains of the oppressed? Certainly not. God denounces the oppressor.

> Woe to him that buildeth his house by unrighteousness and his chambers by wrong (Jeremiah 22:13).

> Woe unto them that decree unrighteous decrees, and that write grievousness, which they have prescribed (Isaiah 10:1).

And, to say nothing of the threatenings—repeated and awful—against the ungodly and oppressing powers, symbolized by the "beast" of Daniel and of the Revelation, we have the striking inquiry of Psalm 94:20:

> Shall the throne of iniquity have fellowship with thee, which frameth iniquity by a law?

Now is it credible that notwithstanding these denunciations, the Most High does still forbid, under penalty of his high displeasure, all conflicts for liberty? That he so far takes under his patronage ungodly governments which despise his law and his Son—as to regard any opposition to their authority as opposition made to his own holy "ordinance" of magistracy? To persuade us of this, we may first demand the clearest evidence.

It is evident that the proper interpretation of this passage depends upon the meaning of the phrase, "ordinance of God." What then is its import? Does it mean any and every government? Does it mean Phocas, who "waded to the throne of the Roman Empire through seas of blood?" Does it mean that Joseph of Austria, with his government, is the "ordinance of God" to Hungary? Does it mean the government of the Pope and his cardinals, under which the Papal States groan? In short, is this term applied to any government merely from the fact that it exists? Clearly not; for, then, the powers just mentioned must be also embraced in it—a conclusion equally repulsive to the Christian and to the friend of human liberty. And, besides, if this be its meaning, the *very worst* government has the very same right to demand unresisting subjection, as the very best, for both alike exist—exist in the same over-ruling and all-controlling providence; and both would be armed with the same high sanction: to "resist" either, would be to make the same assault upon the "ordinance of God!"

What, then, is its import? The reply has been already anticipated.[7] It denotes God's *moral* ordinance of civil government—it refers to such a government as Paul afterwards describes—a government which is "a terror to evil-doers, and a praise to them that do well"—a government that in due measure answers the ends of the institution of civil rule, a government of law, of equity, possessed of moral attributes, and ruling "under God," by whom it has been "ordered," for the execution of high and useful functions.

---

7. See page 16

Who, then, resists? The reply is at hand, and conclusive. He who opposes the rightful exercise of civil rule; he who would attempt the overthrow of just and wholesome authority; he who endeavors to weaken the hands of the "higher powers" in their performance of the trust committed to them: he who rises against the restraints imposed upon the lawless, the profane: he who willfully disturbs the peace, and interferes with the regular administration of justice: for such, and such alone, assail "the ordinance of God." Indeed, we may well ask how this can possibly apply to any but those who invade the good order of the commonwealth by opposing wholesome rule? The end for which governments were established is, surely, more important than government itself, and much more important than the particular form, or the mere fact of the possession of power by this individual or that. How, then, can anyone be regarded as chargeable with the sin and crime of resisting God's "ordinance," who refuses to obey an unjust enactment, or who even goes so far as to attempt the overthrow of or remodeling of a government that is, by tyranny, or injustice, or ungodliness, working harm to society, and dishonor to God, and so tends to defeat the very ends for which the "ordinance" of civil rule was established? The commands of a maniac or drunken father may be disregarded—the wife or even the children taking the government into their own hands— much more may institutions and laws be disregarded when these run counter, either in their constitution or administration, to the divine law, and thus tend to the manifest injury of the commonwealth.[8]

---

8. "Now this being the argument of the apostle, all that we can possibly collect from his injunctions in this place is this: That it is the indispensable duty of subjects to submit themselves to such governors as answer the good end of their institution; to such rulers as he here describes; such as are not a terror to good works, but to the evil; such as promote the public good, and are continually attending upon this very thing." Hoadly, p. 7.

But does not this tend to the enfeebling of the claims of even legitimate authority? By no means. True, all institutions administered by human hands will, necessarily, bear the marks of human imperfection, and it may be difficult, in theory, to draw the line, and say, this much is requisite to constitute a government on which we may inscribe the title "the ordinance of God;" but, in practice, the difficulty will not be often very great—no greater than in many other departments of duty. Surely, we may go so far as to affirm, with confidence, that every "ordinance of God" will acknowledge his claims—

MOSES AND THE TEN COMMANDMENTS

the claims of His Son (we speak of governments in enlightened lands,) and the supremacy of His law, and will *seek* to promote the welfare of all the subjects or citizens.

35

That this doctrine, moreover, is liable to be abused by the lawless, we admit. The opponents of the principle of "passive obedience" encountered the same objection. Says Bishop Hoadly,

> The great objection against this, though it be all founded upon the will of God, who sincerely desires the happiness of public societies, is this, that it may give occasion to subjects to disturb and oppose their superiors. But, certainly, a rule is not therefore bad, because men may mistake in the application of it to particular instances; or because evil men may, under the umbrage of it, satisfy their own passions and unreasonable humors; though these latter, as they are disposed to public disturbance, would certainly find out some other pretence for their behavior, if they wanted this. The contrary doctrine to what I have been delivering, we know, by an almost fatal experience, may be very much abused; and yet that is not the reason why it ought to be rejected, but because it is not true. Every man is to give an account for his sins; and the guilt of those who, under any pretence whatsoever, disturb the government of such as act the part of good rulers, is so great, that there cannot be a stronger motive than this against resistance and opposition to such.[9]

It may be added that every argument on behalf of civil liberty may also be abused, and equally, the doctrines of grace. And yet, after all, we need not much fear any liability to abuse in the application of this principle, provided it be rightly understood; for its very basis and groundwork is that God has ordained civil society and organization, and that existing institutions are only to be resist-

---

9. Hoadly, pp. 10, 11.

ed when they fail to answer the ends for which government has been established among divine ordinances, while—and this is the apostle's argument— to "resist" a government which is really an "ordinance of God" is a sin of heinous character. This is plainly taught when Paul proceeds to enforce subjection,

(2.) *From the danger of resistance.* And they that resist shall receive to themselves damnation, (κριμα—condemnation,) v.2. From what quarter? from the government, or from God? That the apostle designed no more than to assert the fact that such as impugn the authority of government, or resist its commands, or oppose themselves to its authority, will meet with civil punishment, does not appear probable. This would be to assert a fact too well known to require so emphatic and solemn an enunciation. Of course, no government will tamely allow its injunctions to be set at naught, so long as it bears the sword. And, moreover, it seems hardly consistent with the high and religious tone of the entire passage, to understand this clause as having no higher reference than to the infliction of civil punishment upon the disorderly and rebellious. What immediately precedes contains a pretty distinct intimation, as has already been remarked, of the fact that "resistance" to legitimate authority is not only a sin, but a sin of a heinous character. Nor are more express declarations to the same effect wanting elsewhere in the Word of God.

We may refer to the case of Korah and the princes of Judah, whom God visited with a most signal token of his wrath for this very sin. "They went down alive into the pit" (Numbers 16). And all remember the sad story of Absalom, who also died in the same sin in an attempt to overturn a lawful power.[10]

---

10. Hodge says, "Paul does not refer to the punishment which the civil magistrate may inflict, for he is speaking of disobedience to those in authority as a sin

THE DEATH OF ABSALOM

Still, we are not to infer that the sin of resisting civil rule involves necessarily eternal ruin. It deserves "condemnation." God sees it. It highly offends Him. He will vindicate His own "ordinance." And why not? If it be, as it certainly is, a most beneficial one—if it promote directly every temporal interest, and, at least, indirectly bears upon the moral and religious welfare of the community—if successful resistance to good government opens the flood gates to violence, irreligion, vice, and misery—if no interest can flourish when good laws are not well administered—can it be regarded as unworthy of the Divine Spirit to attach this emphatic sanction to the institution of civil rule—to assert, in this explicit form, that God will mark with his evident disapprobation every act of resistance to the righteous exercise of magistratical power?

against God, which he will punish."

CHARLES HODGE (1797–1878)

"Paul does not refer to the punishment which the civil magistrate may inflict, for he is speaking of disobedience to those in authority as a sin against God, which he will punish."

On these high grounds, then, does Paul enforce subjection to the "higher powers." Government is from God—to resist, is to resist his "ordinance," and "he that resists receives a righteous 'condemnation.'"[11]

INFERENCES

1. *That civil government is, as an institution, from God.* National organization is not the mere creature of the voluntary action of the inhabitants of a particular country or district. It is their province, indeed, to establish the particular institutions by which they are to be guided and governed; and in this sense, political arrangements are "the ordinance of man," (1 Peter 2:13). Still, it is not optional with men whether such an institution as civil government exist at all. God has "ordained" it. And it is important to remark, that government once set up, its rights and prerogatives are not *wholly* determined by the popular will. To

---

11. See Appendix C, p. 137

some extent they certainly are; but in others they, as certainly, are not. The Most High has fixed the leading ends of all civil rule;[12] and has also defined, to some extent, the means to be employed in effecting these. It is not optional, for example, with any people, whether they shall commit to the magistracy the power of inflicting death upon the murderer—the law of God determines this. It is a subtle question, and one that in some respects possesses a practical importance—whether civil power is, in the aggregate, a collection made up of contributions of rights thrown in by individual members of the commonwealth—each resigning a portion of his own. By no means. No man has a right to take his own life, and yet society has the right to inflict capital punishment, and, moreover, such a notion is entirely inadmissible on another ground. Man was made for society, and, hence, so far is he from being necessarily restricted in his rights in the social state, that it is as a member of society alone, that he can enjoy all the privileges and perform all the duties of manhood.

In short, while the people of a country have in their own hands the setting up of their government, and the choice of rulers—when this is once done, and *rightly done*—the authority by which the government is administered is to be regarded as derived from the divine institution of the ordinance of magistracy. Hence,

2. The principle standard by which this institution is to be measured is the Word of God. This may be inferred directly from the fact that the scriptures treat so fully on the subject. It appears in each Testament, and in every form of instruction. There are didactic passages—such as that before us. Of this character are the teachings and the precepts of the moral law, which contains a complete exhibition of all that relates to the ends, the principles, the methods of civil rule—and much of the detail respecting

---

12. The fact, and what these ends are, will be the subject of our next section.

magistratical duties, and their correlates, the duties of subjects and citizens. The narratives of the Bible largely illustrate its didactic rules and precepts. It abounds with exemplifications both of good and bad governments, and the issues of the one and of the other. Much of prophecy, both of the Old Testament and of the New, is designed to shed light upon the subject of civil polity, and the divine administrations respecting it.

Where else can this be learned? Not from the light of nature merely. True, the essential principles of social organization, and even of political regimen, are contained in the moral law, and that law is the same that was inscribed upon the heart of man at his creation. But the "law of nature"—the law as a complete rule of human duty is man's primitive condition—the light that is now in man is too feeble to discern it in anything like its holiness and perfection. To reject the Word of God in this, as in any other department of duty, is, to use the words of John Brown of Haddington, "an obstinate drawing back to heathenism."

There is still another reason why we must refer to the scriptures, and make them the supreme standard. There, and there alone, do we ascertain the now essential principle of right civil rule, the Headship of Jesus Christ: for "He is made head over

JOHN BROWN
HADDINGTON
(1722–1787)

"Bearing with the infirmities of the weak, and striving together in prayer, that the word of the Lord may have free course, and be glorified, and your message provided by God, and made acceptable to your hearers"

41

all things to the church" (Ephesians 1:22). To Him "all judgment is committed" (John 5:22). He is "Prince of the kings of the earth" (Romans 1:5). And not merely do we learn this fact, but having ascertained it, we are led at once to the conclusion that to His own Word must we now address ourselves, if we would become acquainted with that institution itself of which He so plainly claims the supremacy.

3. *Disorderly and seditious behavior is here most signally rebuked.* The ordinance of magistracy, rightly set up and administered, ranks among the most important: in some respects, it is first of the institutions with which men have to do. And social order is of itself "of great price." How wrong to disturb it by disorderly and lawless conduct. It is sometimes, indeed, a matter of no little moment to determine were the guilt lies! We would not style any either disorderly or seditious, who are contending in a right spirit against the corruptions of the State, or of the public administration of affairs. Sometimes the rulers themselves are the disturbers of the peace, and upon them falls the threatening of this passage. However, we now speak of the seditious and disorderly, of those who are such in a community where a scriptural magistracy and wholesome rule are in operation. These are to be regarded as chargeable with an offense of no inferior turpitude; as deserving of the most severe reprobation, and as fit subjects for punitive inflictions. And, it may be added, that the spirit of peace and order should, as far as possible, characterize the conduct of those who dissent from unholy and oppressive governments, and attempt their reformation.

3

The Institution of Civil Government

For rulers are not a terror to good works, but to the evil (Verse 3).

This and the subsequent section furnish us with the key to the entire passage. Had the apostle merely enjoined subjection to civil authorities, as he does in the terms of the first and second, adding no explanations, giving no clue to the character of the power to which his injunction is designed to apply, it would have been difficult, perhaps impossible, *from the passage itself*, to have shown any limitations—we might have been compelled to resort mainly to other Scriptures for light as to the duty really, after all, enjoined. We might, indeed, have obtained some light from the term (εξουσια,) and from the phrase (τεταγμενοι υπο του Θεου:) we could have evaded the advocate of "passive obedience and non-resistance," but we would almost have despaired of convincing him. But with the apostle's own explanations all is clear. He enjoins obedience, but he adds a reason drawn from the character of the power, and so limits, most clearly and conclusively, his own injunction: "*for rulers are not a terror to good works, but to the evil.*"

43

1. *Paul here defines a government set up and engaged in attending to its appropriate functions*: "Rulers are not a terror," etc. Hitherto, the subject has been *government*—civil government as a divine institution. Here, for the first time, we meet with a direct reference to magistrates actually employed in administering the affairs of the commonwealth, including, of course, legislators, judges, and executive officers. This change of phraseology is not without design. It is clearly intended to establish a distinction—a distinction existing in the very nature of the case between the *institution* of government and governors themselves. The institution of government is to be studied, governors are to be tried, or if the expression be more correct, the entire character and operations of government, as it actually exists, urges its claim upon the citizen and the Christian.

2. The governors to whom the injunction of Paul applies *"are not a terror to good works."* To what does Paul here refer? to what class of "works?" Does this phrase mean no more, as Tholuck explains it, than such works as are the opposite of resistance and rebellion? Most certainly not. Such an interpretation puts an entirely new meaning upon the phrase "good works," and would, moreover, fix upon the apostle the charge of expressing himself with an unaccountable obscurity and meagerness. Does it mean such "works" as industry, honesty, and the orderly discharge of common, social, and relative duties? No doubt these are included in it. But even this is a very defective interpretation. There must be added, at least, such things as come under the head of common morality.

But we go farther. Paul here speaks, not as a mere heathen philosopher, but as a Christian minister, and an apostle of Christ. What then are "good works?" The answer is clear. They are such as the law of Christ demands: they are all the external results and fruits of the operations of the Spirit of Christ. Among these, as already intimated, will be found all that is comprehended under the name of morals; but they include much more—Sabbath sanctification, the public profession of the name and truth of Christ—His worship, and efforts to advance his kingdom and interest. Thus, "Created in Christ Jesus unto *good works*" (Ephesians 2:10). "'That the man of God may be perfect, thoroughly furnished unto all *good works*" (2 Timothy 3:17). "He that desireth the office of a bishop desireth a *good work*" (1 Timothy 3:1). "Stablish you in every good work and *work*" (2 Thessalonians 2:17). This good work being, in part, what is referred to elsewhere in addressing the Thessalonian church, that from them "the word of the Lord had sounded out." "And he that overcometh and keepeth *my* works unto the end, to him will I give power over the nations" (Revelation 2:26). And, finally, "Blessed are the dead which die in the Lord—that they may rest from their labors, and *their works* do follow them" (Revelation 14:13).

It is not denied that, in most of these passages and similar ones, works of morality are meant; but in some, the immediate and only reference is to "works" peculiarly denominated religious, and in no instance can these be excluded. How can we imagine that Paul departed, in the passage before us, from the current meaning which every Christian attaches to this phrase.[1] Now, to such "works" magistrates—those referred to by the apostle—will not be "a terror." Against such as practice these, he will enact no laws. And does not the principle already taught, that magistracy is the "ordinance of God," abundantly confirm this? It is, in fact, a most serious error,

---

1. "For temporal princes—not to punish men for any works that are good in themselves (like those which the Christian religion enjoin towards God and man,") etc. Guyse *in loco.*

and one that has led to many others, that God has ordained any institution among men, or sanctions any, in which the promotion of his glory as the Supreme Law-giver, and the alone object of worship and religious homage, is not a *chief* end. "The Lord hath made all things for himself" (Job 16:27). And of every people, in a certain sense, does God say, as He said with a peculiar emphasis of ancient Israel, and says of the Church, "This people have I formed for myself, to show forth my praise." This is expressly asserted of the family relation, Malachi 2:15. And as to government, who questions that among the patriarchs, all authority, including what we now term civil, was to be so employed? We cannot conceive of an intelligent and devout patriarch, or subject of patriarchal government, who would not regard the patriarchal authority as given for the glory of God, in the patronage of "good works" of a religious, as well as of a common moral character. And finally, God himself gave a government to his own chosen Israel, and in defining its powers and functions, leaves no doubt that all the "good works" to which this government was not to be "a terror," were works such as have been specified above as those, in part, intended by Paul. In short, there is every reason—the phrase itself—the ends of the institution of government—its history and the direct teachings of the Most High in the institutes given to Israel—to believe that among the works here meant are those that come under the head of religion—religion in its exterior manifestations.

Now, to such, "rulers are not a terror." Such rulers as Paul refers to will so legislate, so judge, so apply law, as that not only the upright and peaceable, but the fearers of God and the servants of Christ, will be subject to no hindrance, exposed to no danger from the civil arm, in their Christian profession and efforts: such rulers will so act as that Christ may be preached, his

PAUL RESCUED BY
GOVERNMENT OFFICIALS

law defended, his authority maintained, his church propagated, without fear of offending "the powers that be."

3. These rulers use their powers for the restraint of evil— "*but a 'terror to the evil.'*" To ascertain the import of the term "evil," we have only to institute a contrast between this clause and the preceding. "Good works" as such works as are appropriate to the honest, peaceable and moral. Of course, "evil works" are such as dishonesty, turbulence, theft, and all gross departures from morality. "Good works" are such as honor Christ, the Sabbath, the Scriptures, and the name and supreme dignity of a Three-one God. "Evil" works are such as are adverse to all these—blasphemy, profanity, idolatry, and Sabbath violation. Can it be possible that an inspired apostle could use this term in any narrower sense, particularly in defining a divine ordinance?

To all these the rulers here meant are for a "terror." They enact such laws, and so administer these enactments, as that all disorder, vice, and open disregard to God and religion may be discountenanced, and, when circumstances demand this, restrained.

Here, again, we may appeal to collateral sources of argument, to the uniform testimony of the Word of God, and to the examples of all enlightened nations. To the former we need only refer. From the patriarchal ages onward until the cannon of Old Testament revelation—none can doubt that divinely approved civil governments, and acts of civil rulers, are of this character—a "terror to evil works;" and in the New, so far as this aspect of national institutions is referred to, we have but the continuation of the same teachings. "The law," says Paul—meaning, in part, at least, the law of God as established among the Jews—"is not made for a righteous man, but for the lawless and disobedient, for the ungodly and for sinners," etc.; and "if there be any other thing that is contrary to sound doctrine." (1 Timothy 1:9–10) Nor has any Christian nation found itself able fully to reduce to practice any other theory. In words, many do, indeed, deny that acts injurious to morality even, and more, that acts hurtful to religion, can rightfully become subjects of cognizance by the magistrate; but just so far as Christian principle has made itself felt, either directly or by tradition, among any people, have they been obliged to conform to the apostle's definition; very defectively it is true, in most instances, but still sufficiently to show that Christian sense and a regard for the general welfare of society, will not be satisfied without some acknowledgement of the principle. Hence, the laws by which the Sabbath is guarded—laws against shameful vices—laws against blasphemy and profanity—or to present the same fact in a more general and more striking form, where is the government that would think itself justifiable in guarding against the spread of acknowledged moral good, as they do of moral evil?

Nor does it weaken the force of our argument, drawn from the practice of nations, that the legislation to which we have referred is affirmed to be only an indirect way of answering what some call the only end of civil rule—the preservation of peace and of property. At all events, it is admitted to be *necessary*: and if necessary, there can be no question whatever that this sort of governmental action was contemplated in the institution itself. So far as our present purpose is concerned, this is enough; for Paul, certainly, did not intend to omit, in his definition of the function of rulers, a class of acts without which they cannot carry on a permanently wholesome administration of affairs.

On every ground, then, we maintain that Paul designs, in these phrases, to furnish us with a summary, but very comprehensive, view of the official character of such rulers as may lawfully claim our conscientious allegiance and subjection. They are such as render themselves "a terror" not to "good works," in any sound sense, but "to the evil" in every sense in which

49

outward acts are so. Such are the "powers" whom "God has ordained"; such he owns as his "ministers"; the resistance offered to these offends him. All this we will find amply confirmed by the Apostle himself when he proceeds, immediately, to apply the general statement to the different classes of citizens in the State, to the good and the bad.[2]

---

2. Inferences will be deduced from this section, in connection with those of the subsequent section.

4

Application for Both Good and Bad Citizens

Wilt thou then not be afraid of the power? do that which is good, and thou shalt have praise of the same: For he is the minister of God to thee for good. But if thou do that which is evil, be afraid; for he beareth not the sword in vain: for he is the minister of God, a revenger to execute wrath upon him that doeth evil (Verses 3 and 4).

In these clauses Paul applies, and, in so doing, more fully illustrates, the doctrines previously taught in regard to the functions of the civil magistrate. He makes this application:

First, to the case of the upright and faithful citizen.

1. *Good conduct will secure certain advantages under such a government as he has described.* V. 3, "Wilt thou then not be afraid of the power? Do that which is good, and thou shalt have praise of the same." The first clause seems to be intended to meet an objection; an objection to this effect: Civil government is armed with terror—it addresses itself to the fears of men—and, hence, it is inconsistent for a Christian to regard it at all. "Well," says Paul, "Wilt thou not be afraid?" *Dost thou wish* not to be afraid? "Do that which is good," and you need

cherish no fear. The law, as armed with penal sanctions, "is not for the righteous man" (1 Timothy 1:9). Such, by the grace of God enlightening and guiding them, are a law to themselves, etc., hence may live, and do live, under just civil rule without fear, at least, without slavish fear—without any such fear as is adverse to unalloyed Christian peace.

And even more, "Do that which is good, *and thou shalt have praise of the same.*" It is not, of course, to be inferred, from this language, that civil government is instituted for the purpose of conferring rewards, in any gross form, upon even the best citizens: still good conduct secures praise; for by an upright, peaceable and Christian deportment, good citizens acquire reputation and influence, and in such a government as Paul describes, this class of citizens, and this only, would be admitted to places of power and trust. These are no mean rewards. It is no inconsiderable result of becoming conduct, that it attracts the favorable regard of the community, and opens the way to seats of more eminent influence.

2. This the Apostle proceeds to *confirm.* V. 4, "For he is the minister of God to thee for good."

We have here a two-fold argument—one drawn from the relation which the magistrate bears to God, another from the end of his appointment.

(1.) *The magistrate is God's servant.* "For he is the minister (διακονος) of God"; and that in a sense, not materially different from that in which ministers are styled (διακονοι) "servants of Christ." They are so, inasmuch as they administer a divinely appointed ecclesiastical constitution, and perform, in Christ's name, duties which he has prescribed, and this for the attainment of ends clearly expressed in the laws pertaining to the church's organization. So civil rulers; for they, also, are called to administer a divine institution for the promotion of the ends contemplated in the ordinance of civil society: the parallel holds in another most important particular. The servant of Christ is, necessarily, under law to Christ, not only as accountable to Him for the manner in which his service is performed, but as the very performance itself is regulated by laws which Christ, his Master, has enacted. So, with some limitations, we assert of the civil ruler. He is not, indeed, furnished with a complete code of laws, but he has sufficiently clear intimations, particularly with the Bible before him, of the will of his master: he is to be "a terror, not to good works, but to the evil." And now the parallel ought surely to hold in another respect. Who will say that that man is a "servant of Christ," even although he occupy the seat, and professes to act in that character, no matter how many acknowledge him, who disregards the law of Christ, perverts the gospel, and tramples on the rights of his people? What Protestant, for example, acknowledges the Pope of Rome as a "servant of Christ?" And yet he has his millions of votaries, and claims to be Christ's vicegerent. *He* is "a servant of Christ," who *serves* Christ. So it is in the case of civil rule. How can he be the servant of God, in administering civil rule, who either denies God's supremacy, or perverts the ends of government, and, particularly, if he also employ his power against God, his law, his gospel, his church and his Son.[1]

But, to return. The magistrate is "God's servant," and hence, it *must* be the end and design of his office to do God's work. God is his Master, whose law, gospel, glory and kingdom the magistrate must seek to promote: as God is a praise

---

1. It is one objection to this that Cyrus is called God's shepherd (Isaiah 44:28). This refers merely to the fact that Cyrus was raised up for a particular purpose. The devil is, in the same providential sense, Christ's servant.

to them that do well, so must the ruler be also, for he is called to act as his servant.

(2.) The magistrate is God's servant for the good of God's people. "The minister of God to thee for good." "To thee!" To whom? To every citizen, certainly. The design of the appointment of civil rulers is, that they may be useful—that they may be employed in securing the rights, the liberty, the safety, the property, of every citizen. As previously remarked, "the civil authority extends its aegis over every person and every interest in the commonwealth." Are we at liberty to exclude the Christian citizen? Assuredly not. Indeed, Paul seems to refer with peculiar emphasis to the godly. To them he addresses this epistle. By what right, then, does anyone undertake to say, that in this phrase Paul alludes only to the citizen, and that, merely in reference to his common social rights? Every rule of interpretation forbids this. We do not affirm that he means the church alone— not even the church directly—but we are assured that it is handling the word of God most unfairly, to exclude the church and the faithful in their character as servants of Christ. And can we conceive it possible that God has set up such an institution, armed with such powers, and yet has done this, without any regard to the safety, the assistance of his own friends, the disciples of his Son, in that great work to which they have been especially and imperatively called? This is impossible: the thought is dishonoring to God. The magistrate is set up that he may guard the rights of every member of the community—protect the weak against the strong—restrain all violence—promote every good work, and so secure the welfare of the whole community; but surely, as God's "servant," he must have a special concern for the name, and cause, and kingdom of God, as these are, in a still higher sense, entrusted to the faithful, and exemplified in them.

But, is this all? Has the "minister of God" fulfilled his whole functions, when he merely secures the religious liberties of the faithful? He has not. He is a "minister for *good*." As God's servant to do his work, he must seek, by some positive acts, the "good" of the friends of God. He must be, in this sense, "a praise" to them that do well. He must give them encouragement and sustain them in their Christian efforts. In a word, he must copy the example of the patriarchs; for, as we have already seen, this was required of *them*. He must copy the example of godly rulers in Israel—as far as the general principle is concerned, for this was required imperatively of them. He must not fall behind even heathen kings, who, like Cyrus, passed decrees and promoted their execution, for the re-building of Jerusalem and the establishment of God's worship.

2. Paul applies the doctrine respecting the ends of government *to the case of bad citizens.* V. 4, "But if thou do that which is evil, be afraid: for he beareth not the sword in vain: for he is the minister of God, a revenger to execute wrath upon him that doeth evil."

In these clauses we have the reverse picture of the action of a right civil government. The same general arrangement is followed—

1. *The Apostle asserts that evil doers have reason to fear its power.* "But, if thou do evil, be afraid." This, no doubt, refers to such evil acts as strike directly at the authority of government, the peace of society and the property, the reputation, or the life of well disposed citizens. But, it embraces more. Unless we are prepared to limit it as neither the word of God nor the practice of enlightened nations warrants, it must be interpreted in a wider sense, so as to include acts committed against the laws of morality—such as profanity, blasphemy, and open dishonor done to God and his Christ—to such as commit these

the faithful ruler is a "terror"; they may justly fear him. This statement Paul,

2. In the second place, confirms: for (1.) *The magistrate is invested with punitive power.* "He beareth the sword." This language is partially figurative. The "sword" is the emblem of the power of civil government to inflict pains and penalties. In this respect, civil authority stands in direct and striking contrast to ecclesiastical; for the latter has no other power than that which appeals to the understanding, the heart and the conscience: it can act by means of admonition, reproof, exhortation, and, in the last resort, can place the erroneous and the immoral outside the pale of the visible church. Civil authority sustains itself and enforces it enactments by penalties of a different sort, when necessary. It uses force, not as the only means of securing conformity to its decrees, for it also may use admonition and persuasion—but, as the last resort, when milder measures fail.

The "sword," moreover, is an instrument of death—for, so far as this even may the magistrate go, in the punishment of signal crimes, either against the State or its citizens. Still, we are not to infer that every crime is to be punished with this extreme penalty. Far from it. The "sword" here is, we repeat, an emblem,—the power of the sword comprehending every grade of penal infliction, from the smallest fine to the severest sort of punishment. Civil rulers are endowed with power to affix and execute suitable penal sanctions.

(2.) *Rulers, such as Paul here intends, will, in this respect, do their duty.* "He beareth not the sword in vain." The righteous magistrate, who knows his place, and has a proper sense of the nature and functions of the magistracy, will not allow the transgressors of law to escape with impunity. He not only "bears the sword"—he is not only armed with a just authority—he will use the "sword:" it will not lie idly in the scabbard; he will exercise the power with which he has been invested. Faithful to his calling and to the great interests of social and moral order, the upright civil functionary, whether in a higher or an inferior station, will not permit God's authority to be impugned, or the interests of society to suffer, from unrestrained lawlessness—from flagrant breaches of the peace—from rampant immorality—from gross, avowed and open hostility to the name and law of God. To be indifferent to these, or to administer law partially, inflicting punishment upon the weak and unprotected, while the evil deeds of the elevated and strong are winked at, is a virtual abdication of power. Such may "bear the sword," but they bear it "in vain." They are no more rulers, as Paul speaks of them, than he is a soldier who neglects or refuses to draw his sword in the heat of conflict: they inspire no "terror"; evil is put under no salutary restraints, "evil" in its worst forms, at least. In short, the magistrate who can claim the subjection here enjoined is no idler; he acts, even in this, the most trying department of his office; for

(3.) *"He is the minister of God."* So Paul has already, in the first clause of this verse, styled the magistrate, but in a different connection—in a different aspect of his functions. Then he considered him as engaged in ministering to the welfare of the good and honest, particularly Christian citizens—here as the minister of God in another aspect, and yet not in any materially different sense. God is good. He is a beneficial sovereign. He has established institutions among men for the good of man; and committed their administration to the hands of men. So far as they come up to the standards, these institutions, in their actual operation, exercise a salutary influence over all who subject themselves to their sway and direction. But God is also just—a righteous law-giver. The divine government gives no countenance of sin: it is ever against it. And, hence, the Most High has invested all his institutions with some degree of restraining power; and has given them laws by which they are to be guided in the disciplinary or punitive department of their functions. In this sense, parents are "ministers of God," in the training of their children—church officers in the exercise of discipline, and, now, we add, civil rulers in the inflictions of penal law. "Servants of God"; for they act by his authority, and are limited and directed by his supreme and sovereign enactments.

But why does Paul introduce this here? Partly to justify the penal administration of law, partly to gain due respect for the magistrate in this responsible and difficult part of his magistratical calling, and partly to confirm the preceding statement, that the magistracy of which he treats will not allow the wicked to pass unnoticed and unrebuked. How can he be, "for he is the minister of God" for good to man. He is also

PAUL IS HEARD BY GOVERNOR FELIX

(4.) *"A revenger—to execute wrath upon him that doeth evil."* Εκδικος—a revenger, or more properly, an "avenger:" for the vindication of law, in its excellence, authority and obligation, is not "revenge," in the sense commonly affixed to that term. Nor does the word properly import this. When Paul speaks of the magistrate as an "avenger," it is in view of the fact that the end of penal sanctions is eminently vindicatory. In this, the civil magistrate is the "minister of God" to whom "vengeance belongs" in its highest and most ample sense—for "He will repay." He has, however, invested the magistrate with a portion, so to speak—a small portion, indeed—of His own ineffable supremacy and power, that he may employ it as His "servant" in the maintenance of the high claims of equity, truth, peace, and purity in the commonwealth; and, that, if called for, he may present before the eyes of the subject or the citizen, examples of the inflexible demands of that law which is "holy" and "just" as well as "good."

If these views be correct, it appears to follow very plainly, that the "wrath" which the magistrate administers implies no *passion* of resentment in the mind of the ruler. This need have no place—in all ordinary cases ought to have none. Remembering the ultimate source of his power, the God-fearing judge or executive officer will calmly, and with no desire of personal vengeance, apply to offenders the punishment which their crimes have *merited*.

The sum of this entire section is—that such magistrates as Paul here means will not be remiss, either in protecting, and fostering the good, or in punishing the bad. They may not, they will not, be perfect. Parents, the best, are not. Ecclesiastical rulers are not. Neither can we look for perfection in civil functionaries. But at these objects good rulers will aim.

Inferences

1. *It is evident that the Apostle enjoins subjection only to such governments as answer the ends of the institution of magistracy.* Great injustice is done to this passage by regarding it in any other way than as a whole. Separate the first and second verses from the context, and they seem to inculcate a blind and complete submission to any authority that may happen to exist. Study the entire passage, and we learn just the contrary. That the constitution and laws and magistrates here meant by the "higher" powers, are such as have for their object the well-being of society, and the glory of God, appears from the connection between the clauses we have now sought to explain, and the Apostle's injunction to obedience. "Be subject—for rulers are not a terror," etc. Otherwise, we must lay to Paul's charge, and to the charge of the Spirit, by whom he was directed, the singular assertion, that every government that can possibly exist is "a praise to them that do well," as Rome, Austria, France! The governments of these countries are all a praise to them that do well—no "terror" these to good works! The truth is, as has been urged before, no reference is made whatever to bad governments or bad magistrates. We here again refer to the great champion of the friends of liberty as against high prerogative in England, from whom we have already quoted pretty largely.

> We may judge, from what I have said, how little ground there is, from anything here delivered by Paul, to argue to so unlimited a submission as some inculcate. For we see he hath his eye all the way upon the end of all government, and founds his precepts upon this supposition that the rulers answer that good end. If they do not, or if they set themselves to contradict it by oppression, violence, and injustice; by invading and destroying the pub-

lic happiness, and by bringing on public miseries; the Apostle seems not to think of recommending submission to the subject. For whilst he commands submission, he puts no case of princes acting contrary to the purpose of their institution, and the sole business of their office, much less of princes who make an express contract with their people, and solemn oaths to preserve their rights and liberties, and afterwards break through all these ties to invade their happiness. Nor doth he mention anything of a passive submission in such cases; but plainly leaves nations to the dictates of common sense and the powerful law of self-preservation; and this under all forms of government equally....

That governor who contradicts the character here laid down by Paul, who is not a terror to evil works, but to good; who is not a minister of good to the virtuous, but of vengeance to the wicked only; and who is not continually watching for the good and happiness of human society, is not the governor whom Paul means in this place, or to whom he here presseth obedience. Can anyone deny that governors are thus described in this place? or that those governors, which are here described, are the governors whom Paul here means? or that this description of his is the argument from whence he presseth subjection in point of conscience? and doth it not follow manifestly from hence, that the governor who contradicts all this description is not the governor here described, and, consequently, not the governor to whom he here presseth obedience? Had it been Paul's design to press obedience to the greatest tyrants and oppressors; or had he had in his eye any particular emperor, who was a monster, not only of villainy, but of public oppression (as some represent his sense;) nothing can be imagined more unaccountable than that he should give such a description of governors as to exclude those whom there was most occasion to mention, and that he should reason Christians into a conscientious subjection in such a manner, as cannot conclude for subjection to any but such governors as he describes in the foregoing words, and as come up to that sense of them in which they should be understood. And if anyone can prove that it is possible he should intend by governors those who are continually attending to the good of their subjects, not only such but also governors who are continually attending and watching to make their subjects miserable; and if anyone can show me the conclusiveness of this argument, rulers are by their office obliged to be a terror to evil works, and not to the good; therefore you are obliged in conscience to submit to them, when they are a terror to good works; then I will retract this sentence.[2]

2. *Civil government should extend it protection to every class, and particularly to the more feeble.* It should be a "praise" to all that do well—a terror to all that do ill. Indeed, nothing can be more certain than that the defense of the poor, of the weak, was one chief object in ordaining civil authority. Surely, it was never contemplated in the divine arrangements in reference to the exercise of civil rule, that it should become, in his name, the instrument of establishing and protecting violence and wrong—in defending the strong in their avaricious, cruel oppression of the destitute and the helpless. That civil

---

2. Hoadly, pp. 9, 21–22. It is but just to state that Hoadly does not *directly* extend the "good works" and the "evil" so far as we have done. With this exception, his exposition agrees with ours. As to the above principle, he goes as far as we do, utterly denying that the mere existence of a government entitles it to obedience.

rulers can prevent all wrong, we are far from affirming—but this they should aim at. If they do the reverse—if they throw their shield over him who deprives his fellow of his rights and liberties, or spoils him of his property—in short, if they sanction such systems as those of serfage and slavery, or even of political oppression, they are not the rulers here designated. And more than this, and still more plainly, if a government deliberately incorporate, among the principles of its constitution, such wrongs, how can it be the ordinance of God for good—or its rulers "ministers of God for good," as Paul here so emphatically styles them? The victims of the wrong may be few comparatively,—they may belong to despised races, but no matter—the government that gives its sanction, knowingly, to injustice—that tolerates so heinous a sin and crime, cannot claim a place among those here meant. It may be free, in other respects—it may allow unlimited scope to the plans and efforts of the *favoured* class; it may be endowed with many attractive features; but if it be the patron of the enslavers of men—if they are crowned with its honors, while the subjects of their ambition, pride, avarice or cruelty, are cast out of the pale of law—and is not this the case even in this land?—such a government stands here condemned.

3. *That many, at least, of the existing governments of the world, have no claim to conscientious acknowledgment.* Try Austria. Is it the good, the God-fearing, the disciples of Christ, that gain for themselves a good name and influence in that Empire? Does the Austrian government prove "a terror" to the immoral, the profane, the impious? These inquiries bear with them, in the mind of every intelligent man, their own answers. True, even Austria does not employ its coercive power against everything good. It permits industry and common honesty, and will restrain the robber and the cheat. But, on the other

hand, does it not forbid the free circulation of the scriptures? Does it not discountenance and prove itself "a terror" to pure religion? Does it not exert a power, professedly from God, to prevent the diffusion of genuine Christianity?

As all know, this iniquitous government lays its hand upon education, upon the church, upon the Bible; it banishes missionaries, it builds up its highest barriers against efforts to bring it millions of ignorant and deluded subjects to the knowledge of "the truth as it is in Jesus." And, still more, its great aim is to prevent free thought, free speech, and the free circulation of intelligence; and it labors, with all authority, to keep down the masses, and subject them to the control of a corrupt and pampered aristocracy. Were Paul—were Christ himself to appear among them, and teach as they taught, bonds, imprisonment and death would await them. In a word, is it the pious, the devout, the energetic Christian to whom this despotic power becomes "a praise"? Nothing of the kind.

How is it with France? The reply is but the repetition of our account of Austria. Famous, indeed, has France been, whether as a kingdom, republic, or empire, for its rejection of Christ, its hatred of his people, its persecution of the faithful.[3] And so, Spain, Portugal, Tuscany, Rome, Russia, and others.

These considerations derive no little weight from the circumstance that is not mere "submission" that is here enjoined—it is active obedience and support. Whatever government Paul means—he demands that it be not merely an outward conformity to its will—but a hearty, conscientious acknowledgment of its claims. Now, surely, the Lord does not demand that we should recognize even these governments as

---

3. The present government is no exception. Protestants are not, indeed, put to death, but they are discountenanced, and the circulation of the Scriptures restrained.

THE FRENCH REVOLUTION OF 1789

his "ordinance"—give them an active homage, and pay them that reverence that is due to his "ministers!" Do not all the friends of liberty earnestly desire their downfall; and all the Christian friends of liberty pray for it? Paul meant no such government. It is ridiculous to attempt to apply his description to such conspiracies against God and man as the governments we have specified, and similar ones, are. They have no place to stand on in this passage—they are "found wanting"—they cannot claim the conscientious obedience of the subjects—they, enemies of God and of man, can impress no sanction, which God will recognize, upon their enactments.

4. *Civil government is instituted for the promotion of moral, as well as social order, among men.* That one, and a leading end of civil government, is to guard the rights of the people;

in other words, that it is designed, not for the rulers, but the ruled, none will, probably, be now disposed to question. It is not so generally admitted—by many it is expressly denied—that this institution of God has anything to do directly with morals or religion. Few are willing, indeed, to go so far as to dispute the existence of, at least, an indirect power in society to cherish the interests of morality—and, perhaps, it would be admitted that religion should receive more countenance than irreligion. But this passage proves more than this. It proves—we think it demonstrates—that there is a direct and specific obligation lying upon civil rulers to have an eye to everything that goes to promote the glory of God, the fountain of all power, and the author of civil rule. They are not only to refrain from everything that would interfere with pure religion and scriptural morality, but to promote well doing—to be "a praise to them that do well," and "a terror" to all evil doers. Nor can it be fairly objected that this would issue in persecution. It is to be remembered that the law of God is their rule, and that, in the exercise of their power, they must be limited by its prescriptions. Unless that law warrants persecution rulers cannot persecute; and, besides, it remains with the objector to show how the patronage of true religion, and the restrain of that which is dishonoring to God and hurtful to his kingdom, can be demonstrated persecution.

5. *Civil rulers are under imperative obligations to recognize the divine supremacy, and that in their official character.* Paul here styles them the "ministers of God"—God's servants. The servant should know his master even among men. And still more should he who professes to wield an authority derived from God, in administering an "ordinance of God," acknowledge, reverence and give due homage to his sovereign. This acknowledgement should be practical. It does not consist in a mere

profession of belief in His being, or even in His providence. It implies the study of His will, and a constant aim and effort to please Him. The ruler, or the nation, that claims to be above all other authority, demanding an unquestioning obedience to mere human law—that denies the existence of a "higher law," is in rebellion against God—is not a "servant," in Paul's sense. And more than this, the acknowledgment must be direct, and in express terms—it must be an acknowledgment—among enlightened people—of the supremacy of the Most High; of his laws, as the Scriptures teach them. Further, still, this acknowledgment must be rendered, not to the God of the deist—but to the only true God—the Christian's God—to God in Christ.

Does the refusal to acknowledge God invalidate the authority of a government as tyranny does? Why not? Surely, if God has ordained this institution for his glory—if he has put it under his law—if he has designed to exhibit in it something of his majesty ("I said that ye are gods"; Psalm 82), it is difficult to see how a government that denies their maker and Lord of all—or withholds from him, from his law, and from his Son, even an acknowledgment, can claim his sanction upon its acts? Surely, God does not threaten with "damnation" those who refuse to bow their consciences before his enemies![4]

6. *It follows, indisputably, from the whole tenor of verses 3 and 4, that civil rulers should be God-fearing men.* Every clause demonstrates this. If a ruler should be a "terror" to evil works, and a "praise to them that do well"—if the magistrate is "a minister of God"—if he is under law to God in his official doings—if his duties are most onerous and responsible, involving the highest interests and dearest rights of the citizen—if his magistratical acts bear, with no little directness and force, upon the interests of morality and religion, surely, rulers

---

4. This subject, and kindred ones, will be taken up in a subsequent section.

should be men of principle, of integrity, of Christian character. There is, in fact, something monstrous in the idea of committing the administration of an eminent divine institution to the hands of the immoral and irreligious: and, if this be done by the vote of the people, can it be otherwise than offensive to the supreme moral Governor? On this point, also, we have the most explicit testimony of God himself:

> Moreover, thou shalt provide out of the people able men—such as fear God—men of truth, hating covetousness (Exodus 18:21).

> He that ruleth over men must be just, ruling in the fear of God (2 Samuel 23:3).

Nor can it be objected that these are Old Testament injunctions. The last is a general statement; equally true—equally obligatory, in all ages. And, though the first was a law addressed to Israel in the wilderness, it is no less binding now than then. It is a declaration of the will of God in the matter to which it relates. No reason can be assigned why it should be regarded as now set aside. Surely, the clearer light which the New Testament sheds upon the things of God, does not diminish either the duty or the necessity of appointing to office none but such as may be expected to honor the supreme law and moral Governor—who will pay due regard to the heaven ordained ends, laws and relations of civil government. Moreover, this law is characterized by divine wisdom. How can it be hoped that the immoral or the irreligious will faithfully administer law? Will such men regard their oaths? The safety of the community demands that the power of legislating, and of judging, and of enforcing law, should be kept out of the hands of the personally ungodly and impure. And, finally, there is no little stress to be laid upon the matter of example.

Application for Both Good and Bad Citizens

We again quote Hoadly:

> To all other qualifications there must be joined a blameless example. The reason is, because everything that tends to promote religion and happiness in a society, is the concern of all who have authority in it. Now, it is with those who are to punish vice and protect virtue, just as it is with those who are to teach the practice of virtue, and the abhorrence of vice. It is an observation, easy and obvious to everybody, that those who are the preachers of righteousness do no great service to the cause; but, perhaps, the contrary, if their examples, unhappily, contradict their precepts. And it is certainly the same with respect to those whose business it is to punish vice. If, whilst they punish it in inferiors, they themselves are known to be guilty of it, the correction, indeed, may make the offender avoid the light; but it will never make him in love with virtue. He will be apt to think he is punished only because he is poor, and not considerable enough to be in office himself; and may be hardened to vice, whilst he sees men making use of their authority in punishing others only, as it were, for a screen to their own greater indulgence.

7. *Government is endowed with the right of inflicting capital punishment.* Of the ruler, it has been said, "He beareth the sword,"—an emblematic expression, but importing, also, literally, a power to take life in extreme cases.

8. *The infliction of penal sanctions by national authorities is not solely for reformation, but, also, and even primarily, for the vindication of the law.* It is not affirmed that the execution of law consists entirely in acts of a punitive character. It would be so, provided government had been established with no other view than to protect the peaceable citizen. Such a

PAUL APPEALS TO CAESAR

notion is most derogatory to the magistrate and the government. The civil ruler would then be no more than a policeman, and government a system of police. Government has higher functions. It is a "praise" to them that do well. And, hence, it takes an interest in all that promotes a quiet, industrious and moral behavior—it provides for the education of the people—it ought to interest itself in the maintenance of pure religious observations.

But, after all, there will be the lawless and the vicious, who must be encountered and kept in awe by the display of the "terrors" of justice. For such characters, and for such ends, mainly, penal sanctions are annexed to law. They serve, indeed, a useful purpose in the case even of the orderly, for none are perfectly free from disturbing passions—but their main use is to alarm those who can be addressed through no other avenue than their fears. The language of the passage before us is most explicit—the magistrate is a "revenger to execute wrath." By inflicting penalties, he exhibits the desert of transgression, and shows that law is, indeed, law—that it is no mere nerveless utterance of the supreme power, but a thing of life and of energy. Still, it needs, also, to be remembered that this vengeance of the law is far from being mere vengeance—it has, even as exercised upon the offender himself, except in the case of capital punishment, a wholesome influence—and, in all cases, it serves as a admonition to others "that they may see, and fear, and do no more wickedly."

5

The Principles of Obedience to Civil Rule

Wherefore, ye must needs be subject, not only for wrath, but also for conscience sake (Verse 5).

This topic has been incidentally noticed in commenting upon the duty itself; but it is made the subject of a distinct statement.

1. *Obedience is to be rendered partly to avoid penal inflictions—"for wrath's sake."* It is not very material to determine whether the Apostle here refers to the "wrath of the magistrate, or of God, or of both." If to the first—and the connection in which the term occurs seems to warrant this view—it still implies that the displeasure of God, also, rests upon him who withholds due subjection from the authorities previously described. It is more important to remark that this phrase has been frequently applied to express that sort of submission which the slave gives his master, or the oppressed to the power of the despot—a submission altogether forced, in which there is no heartfelt recognition. There is such a subjection to lawless authority, and such a submission may be given on this principle. Moreover, this term is appropriate enough as thus applied. But it has not this meaning here. As has been frequently stated

already, Paul refers, in this passage, to no usurped, tyrannical or godless power. He speaks of but one kind of government—one sort of rulers: a government worthy of obedience—rulers who are "ministers of God."

This phrase, as we find it in the passage before us, may be regarded as referring to that class whom we have styled "bad citizens"; for they are kept under only by fear of punishment. But this is not all. The Apostle is addressing Christians—urges upon them a subjection of a different and contrasted character—"not for wrath's sake," but for higher considerations; as much as to say, whatever others may do: *they* may be prompted to conduct themselves peaceably and according to law, only from selfish reasons—but let it not be so with you; you should have another and a better spirit. Still this cannot be the leading object in the introduction of this clause, for this interpretation leaves out of view a very important word. Paul does not barely say "not for wrath's sake"—but, "not *only* for wrath's sake"—intimating that this may be exhibited as a principle of obedience even in addressing the upright citizen. And the subsequent clause confirms this; for, he adds, "but *also* for conscience sake." Nor does this represent the passage as urging a principle unworthy of the Christian. Subjection to lawful authority *merely* for fear is, indeed, radically defective; but such a fear is, collaterally, a lawful principle of action. Hence, in covenanting with Adam, the Most High appeals to this principle: "The day thou eatest thereof thou shalt surely die." In fact, the penalty is essential to the law in the case of all fallible creatures. It is "law" from the very fact that it is armed with such a sanction.

And, besides, it must be remembered that even the best are here imperfect—that they are, in fact, under the influence of corrupt emotions and appetites, and, consequently, require the restraining influence of such considerations as those to which the inspired writer here appeals. God deals with even the faithful as subjects of discipline. He warns them of paternal displeasure in case they sin, and when they do sin, visits them with chastisements. And, finally, the Apostle here brings to view the majesty and terror of civil government, not as belonging to itself alone, but as a transcript, however faint, of the ineffable dignity and eminence of Him in whose name "the sword" is borne and used. In short, there is here presented *one*—though an inferior one—of the principles which move the citizen, or the subject, to a whole-souled obedience to the lawful commands of a lawful power. There is another; for, it is added,

2. *"But also for conscience sake."* All know something from their own experience of the nature and workings of conscience. Philosophers may debate the question, whether it is a distinct faculty, or the result of the operation of certain faculties; but all, learned and unlearned, agree that it is through the action of conscience that man is made to *feel* his accountability to the Invisible and Supreme. It implies, if it does not essentially consist in, the possession of a moral sense; a sense which judges of right and wrong, not by any humanly enacted law, or with reference to the judgment of an earthly tribunal, but in view of a law of divine obligation and the presence of an unseen Judge. As McCosh says,

> We believe it to be an original, a divinely appointed, a fundamental law. Still, though persons could succeed in analyzing it, it would not be less a law. Suppose there is nothing else in the mind, when contemplating moral actions, but the springing up of emotions, still there must be a *Heaven-appointed* law, otherwise the emotions would not be so invariable.

Conscience then has ever an eye, in all its judgments and dictates, to the tribunal of God. But to what particular duty, or aspect of duty, are its judgments directed as it is here introduced by the apostle? An attempt has been made to connect it with the preceding clause; as if Paul designed to enforce a bare heartless submission, for "wrath's sake," to an unjust or a hard government authority, out of conscience towards God.

Now, it is not denied that in case such submission is properly yielded, and we have admitted that in certain instances it may be, it should be yielded with a good conscience. The slave who plies his labor at the bidding of even a tyrannical master, may do this conscientiously—in part, as he regards his condition in the light of an affliction befalling him in the providence of God, and in part, as he may be influenced by a respect to certain other considerations, such as his own comfort, which every man is bound to promote, so far as he can, without sin, in the exemplification of a meek and quiet spirit, even under the infliction of wrong. But to this the apostle makes no reference here. Unless we have mistaken altogether the drift of the passage, that it relates to good governors, it is impossible that he could. And, moreover, Paul does not say, "Submit for fear of punishment, out of conscience towards God:" giving, in the last clause, a reason for the injunction of the first, or a rule to guide in fulfilling it: "*but* we must needs be subject," that is under obedience, "not only for wrath's, but also for conscience sake;" thus assigning not one reason, but two distinct ones. And, finally, this verse is clearly a conclusion from the whole of the preceding exhibition of the nature and functions of civil power. "Therefore," inasmuch as the "higher powers" are "ordained of God"—inasmuch as "rulers are a terror to the evil, but a praise to them that do well"—inasmuch as government is a divine and a beneficent institution, "ye must needs be subject for conscience sake."

The last paragraph embodies the substance of the meaning of this clause. To obey for "conscience sake" is to obey because God *requires* it—because the lawful magistrate is invested with a legitimate authority to administer an ordinance of God's appointment—because the judgment is "the Lord's."[1] And, finally, because a good government is conducive to the peace, the morality, the religious interests of society.

This is the true, as it is a high principle of obedience to civil rule. And, in fact, in the case of good citizens, it is the main reason why wholesome laws are conformed to. Such have respect, not to any mere human arrangements, but to an institution which bears the impress and sanction of God's name, law, wisdom, supremacy, and majesty. Wherever these are seen, the homage and allegiance of the godly are sincere and genuine. They yield no mere outward and constrained service. What they do as members of the commonwealth, they do, "as to the Lord, and not unto men."

Remarks

1. *It is not left optional with men whether they support righteous civil institutions or not.* We mean as before God. That the citizen may—that he must—"prove" civil institutions and laws, has already been inferred from the preceding statements and reasonings of this passage. But having proved these and found them endowed with the attributes of God's moral ordinance of magistracy—having proved the magistrates themselves, and the design and tendencies of their administration, and approved them, he is not at liberty to withhold the outward tokens of his approval. "Conscience" has to do with it. It has to do with Him who is "Lord of the conscience."

---

1. Second Chronicles 19:8. Of course it is not meant that the magistrate is infallible, but he acts with God's sanction in so far as he acts rightly.

2. *All obedience to civil authority is limited by the higher allegiance due to God its author.* To imagine otherwise is to annihilate, by the law of God, it own authority and sanctions. All right subjection to civil rule regards it as the creature of God, but *no more.* It surely does not give it God's place. Indeed nothing can be more absurd than the notion that "conscience," which always sees God as supreme in His claims and power, should, for a moment, substitute any "lower law" for His. This would be to deny its own nature—to act in direct opposition to the very law of its being. And, hence,

3. *Every attempt to establish a paramount claim for any mere human enactment is really, under the pretence of doing honor to government, to imperil the stability and efficiency of all authority.* What could any government do—unless one of mere force— without the aid and cooperation of the principles of conscience? And what do they seek to accomplish, who deride "The Higher Law," but to sap the very foundations of the social state? Instead of being the friends, such men are the very worst enemies of civil government. Could they absorb the conscience of the individual, and deprive him of the right and the disposition to judge for himself, in the light of God's law, and supremacy, and word, they would but make a community of the very lowest order of slaves, and thus sow the seeds of inevitable disorders and revolutions. They, and they alone, are the friends of civil law and social order, who vindicate the paramount claims of the Supreme Potentate, and maintain the rights of an enlightened conscience. Hence,

4. *May be ascertained the reason why the nations are so generally dissatisfied, and that the more as knowledge increases, with existing governments.* It is because they find in them so little that bears the stamp of rectitude of aim; so little that bears the impress of the divine majesty. True, there are the lawless—the vicious—who, under any administration, would require the exer-

cise of a restraining hand. The discontent we refer to is not only of such. It is that of the thoughtful, the intelligent, the benevolent, the devout. Their dissatisfaction may not always make itself manifest, but it is not the less real. It appears in the withdrawing of many good men from all active concern in politics, and in the longing of the pious for the coming of a time when iniquity shall no longer find refuge under the wings of power—when the legislators and executive officers of the nation shall be trustworthy men—when the entire workings of the social fabric shall be eminently conducive to the promotion of individual and national weal. It will be well for the world when civil government shall be avowedly restored to the domain of conscience—conscience toward God, His law, His Christ, and His gospel.

6

The Duties of
Subjects and Citizens

For this cause pay ye tribute also: for they are God's ministers, attending continually upon this very thing (Verse 6).

Thus far the duty of subjection has been stated in general terms, and pressed upon general considerations. The apostle now proceeds more in detail.

1. The requisite contributions are to be made for the maintenance of government.

The word here rendered "tribute" (φορους) signifies, literally—as does our word by which it is rendered—the contributions levied upon a conquered state or province. It also means any direct tax laid indiscriminately upon all citizens—such as land tax, capitation tax, or a tax upon personal estate; and, even more generally, any kind of levy by which national revenues are gathered, with the exception of customs. This is its meaning here, and the payment of such taxes is enforced by a three-fold argument—and,

(1.) From the nature, and ends, and benefits of civil rule. "For this cause pay ye tribute." Some expositors regard this clause as referring to the preceding verse, and, consequently, as urging a conscientious response to the pecuniary demands of government. To this interpretation there can be no doctrinal objection. This is, in fact, the very gist of the precept contained in the entire verse. It is better, however, to consider this clause as looking back to the whole of the foregoing teachings of the apostle on the subject of civil power and its exercise, with special reference to the great argument which lies at the foundation of the general duty of subjection—the fact that civil government is no mere human arrangement, but a divine institution.

(2.) The apostle argues from the fact that magistrates are God's "ministers." That they are so, has been previously stated, and the import of the term we have attempted to explain, viz., that it designates civil rulers as the servants of God, not in the general way in which all things, even inanimate, serve Him, inasmuch as they are controlled by His power, and guided by His hand, so that they are instruments of accomplishing his unalterable purposes; but in a limited and specific sense, as they are employed in administering his law, in administering authority which He has ordained, in executing functions which he has prescribed. In other words, magistrates are God's "ministers," in a sense analogous to that in which ecclesiastical functionaries are "ministers" of Christ. This view is clearly expressed by the term here rendered "ministers." It is not the same with that used in the fourth verse. There it is διάκο—νος here it is λειτουργοι—a title given by the Athenians to those employed by the state in particular offices by national appointment, and often used by the inspired writers in the sense of holding a public office or ministry. In Hebrews 10:11, it denotes the exercise of the priestly office. The occupant of civil power—by whatever form of lawful procedure invested with power—is still the "minister" of God. To withhold such contributions as the exigencies of the government require, is, consequently, a dishonor done to God, by whom the magistrate has been appointed and his duties assigned.

(3.) The payment of taxes is a duty inasmuch as they are justly due—due upon the principle of work done, and benefit conferred. "Attending continually upon this very thing." Not the collection of taxes merely. It is impossible that this can be the apostle's meaning. Civil rulers are not *mere* tax gatherers. And those who are specially employed in this department are principally of that class to whom, least of all, the passage refers. The magistracy—a good magistracy, and the apostle speaks of no other—"attend" to higher duties, to the advancement of the public weal, the promotion of peace, of social and moral order, of religion, of the glory of God. On this ground, then, it becomes a duty to contribute conscientiously to the national funds. There is a service rendered—a work done—benefit received; and on the common principles of equity which regulate all matters of a pecuniary kind in common intercourse and business.

It may be regarded as strange that this—as we would probably regard it—inferior civil duty should thus be made to occupy the first place in the detailed exhibition of what is comprehended in "subjection" to the "higher powers." Further reflection shows the wisdom of this arrangement; for while the moral and industrious—good citizens—and such as are here mainly addressed, though the duty of all is taught—will not be easily drawn into any course of conduct adverse to social order, it is by no means so easy, even for such, to bear in mind the fact that taxes are to be conscientiously paid—that to defraud the public revenues, directly or indirectly, is to sin against God—not only on the ground and for the reason that it is sin to withhold from any what is their due, but also for the specific reason that the magistrate is God's "minister," and that thence it is a kind of sacrilege to refuse to contribute to the public treasury.

Having, for some such reason as we have assigned, presented this duty, separately and distinctly, Paul proceeds,

(2.) *To present, in one view, the whole range of duties owing to civil rulers.*

> Render, therefore, to all their duties; tribute to whom tribute; custom to whom custom; fear to whom fear; honor to whom honor (Verse 7).

The Subject is still that of civil rule, and, hence, the first clause, which in its terms admits of a wider extension, is limited to the general subject of the passage: "Render to all" in authority "their dues;" for among the "higher powers" some are employed particularly in one department, and some in another. Let each receive that sort of subjection which his peculiar place renders especially imperative. And,

(1.) As before, "Tribute to whom tribute." (2.) "Custom to whom custom." The rendering here is literal and exact. The word used by the apostle (τελος) has precisely the signification here given it. It denotes that sort of revenues which is gathered by impost laid upon property imported from other nations—as tribute (φορος) comprehends all kinds of revenues raised within the national boundaries. (3.) "Fear to whom fear;" meaning not a slavish fear, but that awe which a righteous administration of power is designed and calculated to awaken in the mind of the subject of civil rule; such an awe as leads to a quiet and orderly obedience to the law and its appointed judges and executors. (4.) "Honor to whom honor;" for the magistrate, worthy of the name, deserves, "for his work's sake," as occupying a high place as God's "minister," a peculiar esteem, regard, and homage. His person

84

should be treated with respect, and his faithful administration of law should secure to him the unfeigned respect of the citizen and the Christian. And this, not only for his office's sake, or his work's sake, but as essential to the due influence of his authority in the restraint of the disobedient and the lawless. For, if "honor" be not paid him—if his attempts to vindicate just law, and to advance the public interests, be not sustained by the good opinion of the order-loving portion of the community—if they indulge in contempt of his person, it is evident his authority will be little feared by that class of the population which especially requires the control of sound legislative and judicial action. It was a precept of heavenly wisdom, "Thou shalt not speak evil of the ruler of thy people."

We have said the magistrate "worthy of the name;" for neither reason nor scripture demands or even justifies the rendering of honor to the tyrannical, the immoral, the profane, the godless. Reason does not; for this would tend to confound all moral distinction. To honor the undeserving is contrary to every right feeling—to every intelligent conviction; for what claim to "honor," as "the minister of God," has one like the present Emperor of France—a licentious, godless adventurer, elected by craft and violence to his seat of power; or a Pius IX the occupant of a blasphemous throne—the deceiver and oppressor of his ruined States—the prime leader in Satan's grand array against Christ and his gospel? Such may wear the crown—they may shine in purple or in scarlet—they may receive the homage of the pliant and interested tools of their base conspiracies against God and man,—but right reason forbids us to regard them with that "honor" which the power "ordained of God" may justly demand.

The Scriptures most clearly sanction what in this matter reason teaches. Saul was king of Israel; but, at the same time,

SAUL SUMMONS SAMUEL

he was a rebel against God and Samuel, the Lord's prophet, thus addressed him,

> "I will not return to thee; for thou hast rejected the word of the Lord, and the Lord hath rejected thee from being king over Israel." (1 Samuel 15:26)

And Elisha, born within the limits of the ten tribes, not only withheld all tokens of "honor" from their idolatrous king, Ahab, but publicly denounced him as unworthy of the notice of the Lord's prophet:

> As the Lord of hosts liveth, before whom I stand, surely, were it not that I regard the presence of Jehoshaphat the King of Judah, I would not look towards thee, nor see thee (2 Kings 3:14).

And our Lord himself, speaking of Herod, says,

> Go ye, and tell that fox, "Behold, I cast out devils, and I do cures today and tomorrow, and the third day I shall be perfected" (Luke 13:32).

"Honor" is too precious to be lavished upon the base, the godless, the cruel.

CHRIST ENCOUNTERS HEROD

Remarks

1. *Common, everyday duties are to be performed religiously.* This is clearly implied in the whole strain of the verses before us. They embrace the discharge of *all* civil duties, the whole subject of obedience to the law; and the motives by which these are enforced are, throughout, religious. That is not true religion whose practical influence extends no farther than acts of devotion, or to relations merely domestic and ecclesiastical. Genuine piety and godliness are all-pervading. The *heart* of the truly devout is, in every principle, in every emotion, in every purpose, quickened and renovated by a new and energetic life; a life possessed of such properties as necessarily constitute it a universal principle of action.

> If any man be in Christ, he is a new creature—old things are passed away; behold, all things are become new (2 Corinthians 5:17).

Hence, even the making of pecuniary contributions for the maintenance of government, is an act to be performed with an eye to the law and authority of God, as the *prime* consideration. That sort of religion which confines its guiding and restraining influence to *any* limited sphere should not merely be suspected but denounced. The sincere Christian will be a Christian in the mart of business, in the hall of legislation, in the seat of science, in the executive chair, and in the walks of social intercourse. He stands ever in direct contrast with the godless—for "God *is* in all his thoughts," and he is bound by, and *ought* to feel the obligations of the divine law and the responsibilities of the Christian character, in every place, relation, and act,—and can, of course, no more sanction or do anything to sustain error, heresy, or wrong, blasphemy, idolatry, or oppression, Socinianism, popery, or slaveholding, when employed in civil or political functions, than in the family, the sanctuary, or the court of ecclesiastical judicature. Hence,

2. *It is equally clear that all civil duties are to be done with reference to Christ as the administrator of the law of Heaven.* It is admitted that the passage before us makes no direct allusion to Christ as the medium of all true and acceptable obedience to God. But this is not the less implied. If magistrates are to be "feared" and "honored" devoutly and religiously, it must be in Christ. Moreover, we may and ought to compare Scripture with Scripture. One passage—as this—enjoins duties, and states the general principles on which they are to be performed: other passages exhibit the precise form in which the service is to be rendered. Turning to these we find their light and teaching clear and explicit. The Master himself says:

> No man cometh to the Father but by me (John 14:6).

And again:

> The Father judgeth no man, but hath committed all judgment to the Son, that all men should honor the Son, even as they honor the Father. He that honoreth not the Son honoreth not the Father which hath sent him (John 5:22–23).

And finally, speaking by Paul:

> And whatsoever ye do, do it heartily as to the Lord, and not unto men, knowing that of the Lord ye shall receive the reward of the inheritance, for ye serve the Lord Christ (John 14:6; 5:22, 23; Colossians 3:24, 25).

3. *The Scriptures are a complete and perfect rule of obedience.* The main design, indeed, of divine revelation is to teach

men their condition and state before God, and to lead them back, by the discoveries they make of the glory, majesty, supremacy, holiness, and mercy of God, to Him as the fountain of life, the only source of permanent blessedness. They also reveal the fact that in a future state the common relations and occupations of the present state shall have no place, and yet it is apparent in every part of the sacred volume that it is designed to shed its light upon every one of these so long as they are to engage the attention of men, and to enforce, even here, exclusive devotion of mind, heart and effort, to the service of God. It is a plausible but very superficial view of the Book of God, and its design, to imagine that it slights the affairs of time, as utterly unworthy of its regard in comparison with things eternal. The truth is, the law—the revealed will and law of God—covers the entire existence of man, and is intended to furnish all the instruction requisite for the right exercise of every faculty, the right use of every gift, in whatever condition and circumstances, man, the creature of God, is placed by the hand of his Maker, and also to enforce its instruction by the paramount authority of Him who is the "only Potentate."

So far then is it from being true that the Christian is to disregard the movements of society, or even what relates to matters of civil regimen, and human rights and liberty, that the very opposite is a truth, and a most important one. The Christian should, of all men, regard things like these with a constant and active interest. So his Bible teaches him—for its pages abound in directions bearing immediately upon them. So soon as he opens its pages, his eye lights upon some truth, law, maxim, warning or example, which he may and should apply to the ordinary interests of time. Hence,

4. *The Bible is the great security of all social order.* The Bible, of course, read, studied, believed, and made "the man of our

counsel." It must be so; for it guards on the one hand, when fairly interpreted, the rights of the individual; it allows of no tyrannical exercise of power, forbidding all oppression, and elevating every human being to his true position of dignity and worth as intelligent and immortal; bringing all down to the same level as guilty before God, and utterly alienated from Him; raising again all the penitent and the believing alike to the highest place of privilege and of hope. Consequently it abases pride, restrains gross and vulgar ambition, teaches mutual esteem, and enjoins mutual interest and good offices.

But on the other hand, the Bible enforces with its sanctions a due arrangement, connection and subordination in human society. Ever maintaining the prerogatives of an enlightened conscience, it offers no toleration to the vicious, the malevolent, the disorderly, the seditious. It not only restrains them by clear discoveries of the wrath of God, which inevitably attends and visits lawlessness and crime, but, in addition, arms lawful authority with the right to inflict punishment proportioned to the nature and circumstances of offenses against social order and moral law. It establishes all just authority; parental, ecclesiastical and civil.

These properties of the Word of God, properly considered, enable us to see why it is that tyrants fear it; that despotic governments oppose its free circulation. It sets up a standard of judgment as the guide of human action infinitely above the enactments of mere human power. It divests man of a superstitious and debasing reverence for arbitrary rule. It exalts, as to the greatest and most desirable issues, the poorest and humblest to a level with the highest. It brings all alike before the same just and impartial tribunal. And, hence, a community imbued with scriptural knowledge can never become the prey of arbitrary power. Such a people will scorn and cast off the yoke of ignoble bondage. But for the same reason, the Bible ever imparts an unshakable stability to free and equitable social and political arrangements, for it teaches men their several duties, discloses to them the beneficent ends of governmental institutions, and endues them with the dispositions and sobriety requisite to, and that go to make, a stable order of society. The free seek and promote, as the best safeguard of liberty, the knowledge of that very Bible which the aristocratic and selfish would put under restraint.

All history confirms these views, and hence the instructive lesson: study, spread, reverence the inspired volume, for in it we have this life, as well as life eternal.

7

Objections Answered

Our interpretation has brought out very distinctly the principle *that no immoral civil power can demand, at least from any of Paul's teachings in this passage, the conscientious allegiance and subjection of the citizen.* This principle does not meet with ready acceptance. Many who admit, and teach that the obedience due to human authority is in every case to be limited to things in themselves lawful—that is, not contrary to the law of God—do still insist that even in the case of an immoral government—a government, for example, that sanctions or practices oppression, that refuses to acknowledge the Most High, his law and his Son, that sustain false religion, or gives its influence to corrupt forms of Christianity, that winks at and protects flagrant idolatry, that is administered, mainly, by ungodly men; still even such a government is to be recognized as God's, and as such to be obeyed for "conscience sake." The advocates of this principle are neither few nor un-influential. They comprise a very great majority, not of the godless alone, who view all things irrespective of their moral aspects and character, but also of the members and ministers of the Christian churches. Indeed, the opposite opinion, that which we have drawn from the passage, as at least fairly implied in it, is regarded as extreme and fanatical. To this, then, we will direct some attention, and will likewise endeavor, in this connection, to vindicate the truth of our leading principle in the interpretation of this passage.

It is, surely, rather an ungracious task for any Christian to undertake to defend the principle that God recognizes as exemplifications of His ordinance of civil rule, governments of such a character as most of those now existing on earth— to teach that Christ, by his apostle, has enjoined obedience to civil powers, irrespective of their moral character—that whether a government accords with the divine institution of magistracy, or not, it is to be honored as God's—that the thunderings of divine wrath against those who "resist" authority are directed equally against such as refuse to acknowledge God-forgetting and man-oppressing authorities, and those who endeavor to overthrow or bring into contempt such as are based upon righteousness, and are administered with equity and in the fear of God. Yet such expositors there are.

1. *Some assert that the command to be subject is unrestricted, and unlimited.* Says Haldane, "They [Christians] are bound to obey not good rulers only, as Dr. McKnight unwarrantably limits the word, *but oppressive rulers also.*"

> The people of God ought to consider resistance to
> the government under which they live as a very awful crime, even as a resistance to God himself.[1]

The only limitation he admits—the only excepted case—is when a government commands a sinful act.

It is unnecessary to enter here upon a very minute examination of these singular assertions. The age will not bear them. The voice of suffering humanity is raised against them, and true piety revolts at such a partnership in iniquity and wrong, as such a doctrine charges upon the Most High. However, we

---

1. Commentary on the passage.

remark, (1.) If this were true, then Moses and the Israelites did an immense wrong in setting themselves against Pharaoh. The Israelites had gone voluntarily into Egypt—and had been long—for some centuries—under the Egyptian government. What then? Did God send Moses to excite a lawless sedition, to heap dishonor upon a government stamped with his own authority? If not, then have we a clear instance of a lawful tram-

PHARAOH

pling under foot of unjust power—a righteous refusal to obey a government under which the Israelites had been born and reared. (2.) This writer, and he is not alone, makes no distinction between a government which exists in God's providence merely, and a government which accords with His will, and answers the ends, in due measure, of His institution of magistracy. Let Haldane's principle be universally applied, if applied at all: let no resistance be made to the robber, or the midnight assassin; for the same providence permits—the same providence is concerned in their assaults and bloodthirsty violence, as in "raising up" a Pharaoh or a Nero.

NERO CLAUDIUS CAESAR
(AD 37–68)

(3.) Such an interpretation runs counter, among others, to the following passage of Scripture: "Shall the throne of iniquity have fellowship with thee, which frameth mischief by a law?" (Psalm 94:20).

2. *Some assert that the only government that may be lawfully resisted is one tyrannical and oppressive;* that is, if a government regard the common rules of equity in its laws and administration, it is to be obeyed for conscience's sake, let its character otherwise be never so godless. On this we remark, (1.) *That* it admits the property of applying some test to existing institutions. It abandons the principle of unquestioning subjection to any and every existing institution. For, once admit that character is to be looked after at all, and we not only establish a new rule as our guide,

but we absolutely discard, *ipso facto*, the doctrine that a merely providential existence is to be regarded in the matter. If it should, it avails the oppressor as well as the benefactor who occupies the throne and holds the scepter; for the same *providence*, we repeat, has brought both into being, and invested them with the functions and insignia of power. Moreover, the admission, and we believe it is now generally made, is one of no little practical moment. By use of this test, we at once set aside as God-given and reverend, such governments as the Austrian, the Russian, the Tuscan, the Neapolitan, the Papal, the Turkish—and, in a word, all the despotic, and Popish powers of the old world and the new. Nor will the government of this land bear well this test. A constitution that throws its shield over the crime of slave-holding, which puts, to nearly all intents and purposes, three millions of its population out of the pale of its protection, surrendering them to a bondage tenfold more bitter than that of Egypt, has need to tremble lest the doom of the oppressor overwhelm it. (2.) The objection overlooks the fact that this passage describes a moral government.

That the passage does so, we have already endeavored to show. It exhibits a magistrate ruling as God's minister, administering laws which countenance good works and discourage the evil. It is an exceedingly unfair interpretation that would present the apostle as defining civil government as concerned only about breaches of the public peace. The common sense of all enlightened communities repudiates such an exposition. Hence the encouragement given by such to science; the institution and support of schools and colleges, and kindred efforts for the promotion of the public intelligence: and direct efforts also—as in legislation against intemperance and its causes—in behalf of morals. No government among a professedly Christian people has yet been able or, perhaps, disposed, to fall into the limits which *in theory* certain expounders set around it.

But by what right does anyone assert that a practical vindication of human rights is sufficient to render a government valid, while it utterly neglects the acknowledgment of God and of his Christ? or if it names Him, does so merely, or mainly, to establish its own claims, while practically regardless of Him? or, perhaps, while professing to honor Christ, gives its sanction and aid to some corrupted form of Christianity, or to anti-Christ himself? or, finally, which puts true religion and false, Christ and Belial, on the same level? Surely that cannot be "the ordinance of God," which gives to God no such honor as he claims—nor that ruler "the minister of God," who distribute his favors alike, in his political regimen, to the faithful disciples of Christ, and the votaries of the "Mother of harlots." And still more plainly, how can that government be God's, which makes no reference to His law, as of paramount authority, but claims for itself absolute supremacy?

We *must* take the character of the government into the account—its character as here described—in making up our judgment upon this matter of subjection, its limits and re-

ROBERT HALDANE
(1764–1842)

"Every one, without exception, is, by the command of God, to be subject to the existing powers, whatever were the means by which they became possessed of the situation in which they stand."

strictions. Gross injustice has been done the inspired writer by such authors as Haldane, in neglecting this plain canon of interpretation. And here it may be asked, How can we account for it that the class of expositors with whom we have now to do, *leave out*, or give little weight to the very circumstance which Paul himself adduces as a main proof of the duty of subjection, the equity, industry, and discriminating character of the magistracy, and *introduce* another—the will of the people—which is not referred to here in words, at all? The only account we can give of this most flagrant inconsistency is, that advocacy of free government is now popular, while the law of God, and the supremacy of Christ, are as much hated as ever. In an age when human rights were little heard of, none of this class of interpreters said anything about such a limitation. In this age, when the language of men and nations is, "We will not have Christ to reign over us," the true *point* of the passage is slurred over, or misinterpreted. We cannot so "handle" the Word of God. It would look too much like that "deceitful handling" of divine revelation which Paul repudiates and condemns (2 Corinthians 4:2) That the consent of the people is necessary to render a government legitimate, we strenuously maintain; but this passage makes no reference to this aspect of the question. It deals with the duty of subjection, and by a very clear and comprehensive exhibition of the true nature, functions and *character* of government, both enforces and *limits* the duty.

3. *It is objected that even governments, in the main bad, still do some good, and are better than none, and that, hence, they are to be respected and obeyed.* We have already admitted that absolute perfection is not to be looked for in any government framed and administered by human hands, and that, of course, the want of it is not enough to invalidate the authority of a magistracy. Nor do we attempt to draw a theoretical line

of distinction, so distinct and definite, as to rid the settlement of the question regarding the validity of any particular government of all practical difficulty. It is here as it is in reference to the Church. Her constitution, as it lies in the Word of God, is perfect; but defects still exist in the best churches. And it is far from easy—is it possible?—to prepare a minute statement of the marks of a true church, which will render easy the task of deciding in *every* case, absolutely and *at once*, whether a society can be reckoned a true church or not. And yet every intelligent Christian admits that a church, once genuine in its character, may become completely apostate. To draw the line and say, just *here*, it ought to be abandoned, is not easy. The truth is, all questions of this sort must, as they occur, be left for decision, under the guidance of general principles, such as those to which reference has already been made frequently in these pages, to the enlightened judgment, pure hearts, and honest purposes of the faithful in Christ.

But, to come to the objection, we remark: (1.) That the objection proves much more than the objector would himself be willing to admit,[2] for no government ever has, or could exist, that did *no* good to any portion of the community. The most rampant tyranny must have its instruments. These will have their affairs guarded, and their disputes and controversies settled, and, perhaps, fairly. Even a band of pirates cannot dispense altogether with justice. If the doing of some good constitutes a valid claim to allegiance, then resistance to tyrants is not according to the current maxim, "obedience to God," but, *in every case*, arrant and damnable rebellion. The objec-

---

2. We make no reference here to such expositors as Haldane. He would carry out the objection to the farthest extreme. We have in our eye the great mass of the upholders of existing governments, and particularly that portion of those with whom we are in closer contact.

tion proves too much. Every friend of liberty rejects it. (2.) It takes for granted, which is not true, that the removal of a bad government must be succeeded by anarchy. This is impossible—for any appreciable length of time any how. In every revolution provisional authorities are at once established, and their character will be determined, and their policy controlled, by the character and the object of the revolutionists. They *must* organize, and one of their first aims will always be to remove the causes which gave rise to a desire for a change of the government. Abuses may follow, as did in the French Revolution of 1789; but these will find their correction; for society cannot long remain unsettled, nor will it long, when it has the power

FRENCH REVOLUTION OF 1789

in its own hands, tolerate gross evil against its own order and quiet. But still more. That class of citizens, who can alone be regarded as wishing to remodel a godless government, must be guided by a regard for God and his rights. If they should withdraw from an active cooperation with existing institutions, it will be mainly for the purpose of introducing Bible elements into the affairs of state. *They* will not tolerate anarchy.

Nor can it be said, that after all, so long as the government exists, it evils are compensated by its good; that it still furnishes such a degree of protection to the citizen as to warrant and require him to own its claims. True, the state of things may be such that the immediate duty of the faithful may be to do no more than withhold allegiance—laboring in the mean time to establish in the minds of all, governors and governed, sound principles on the subject of social and political arrangements. This may even be acknowledged to be the course generally marked out for them by God's word and providence. But, surely, if the community can be rightly taught, and have been taught to understand their duty, and admit it, no reason can be given why the requisite steps should not at once be taken for making the desired change. A new order of things may and ought to arise.

Hoadly was pressed by the same objection in his controversy with the advocates of "passive obedience and non-resistance." He thus replies:

> There would be some color in this objection, were there no middle condition between tyranny and anarchy, or were it impossible to oppose princes without running into a lawless and ungoverned condition. But I see no necessity of any such thing. And supposing that sometimes a people had, (through the bad designs and evil dispositions of some men,) thrown

off tyranny, and run into confusion, or to a tyranny as bad as the former, this is no reason why any people should endure a present tyranny. For this unhappiness doth not necessarily follow, in the nature of the thing, but is purely accidental, and may, with prudence, be prevented—and they must answer for it who are the causes of it. This is just as the church of Rome would affrighten Christians from the most just separations, by telling them that any church tyranny is better than infinite confusion and numberless separations, which are seen to follow without stop, when separation on any account is allowed of. If it be said here, as it may be by some, that any church tyranny is indeed better than separation, which brings confusion with it,—but we are not here left at liberty, for sinful terms are imposed upon us, and we cannot enjoy the means of public worship without complying actually in sin, and therefore there is a necessity of separating, which cannot be said in the case of resistance. If this, I say, be replied, I answer, first, that we see from hence that a practice may be lawful, notwithstanding that the consequence of it be confusion and anarchy: and then what doth this objection, taken by itself, signify towards proving my doctrine false?

And in the next place our separation, or reformation, with all its consequences, is better than a passive submission to the exorbitant power and tyranny of the Church of Rome, even supposing no terms of external communion absolutely sinful imposed upon us. For as it is exercised in manifold, notorious and scandalous instances, who can prove submission to it to be so much as lawful? And therefore, thirdly, who can prove it so much as lawful to pay such a submission to any mortal upon earth, as helps to ruin and destroy the rights of others, which we cannot honorably give up?

Though we may surrender our own, we cannot surrender the rights and happiness of our neighbors, of all our countrymen, and of all posterity to come. This must be proved by other arguments. But the making this objection is only just, as if one should say to a man dying of a fever, you may indeed be cured of this disease by some particular remedies, but you had better let it take its course, for sometimes it hath been seen that when they have removed that distemper they may have thrown the patient into another as bad, or worse, by pure accident, and through want of due care and prudence. In fine, it doth not in the least follow that because the guarding against one evil hath sometimes accidentally, and without any necessity, brought on another, therefore we may not, in prudence, defend ourselves against it, when we may likewise, if we be not wanting to ourselves, keep off the other also. But were the doctrine I have taught universally and publicly embraced, I am persuaded the ground of all such objections would be removed, because the whole foundation of tyranny would be destroyed, unless where there is supposed a force sufficient to bear it out.[3]

(3.) If this objection be true, no revolution could ever occur, for surely, before any can attempt a radical change of government, and this is the case supposed—they must have previously become convinced that the existing authorities have no claim upon their conscientious support. Take, the English Revolution of 1688. Before adopting measures for the expul-

---

3. Hoadly, pp. 75–77.

sion of James II, the leaders in that transaction must first have seen it to be their duty to refuse him their allegiance. Had they still regarded him as God's "minister," they could not have laid their plans—with a good conscience—to remove him from the throne. And, yet, even then, who can question that James' government yielded much good to the British nation, in the way of preserving peace, and in guarding the private interests of the people of England. And, now, we add, had this revolution failed, would its abettors have become bound to return,

CHARLES II AND JAMES II IN A DEPICTION OF THE
ENGLISH REVOLUTION OF 1688

in heart, to their allegiance? All the reasons would still have existed by which they had been fully satisfied that a revolution was necessary. Would they have been bound to discard their previous judgment? Certainly not. Success or failure in a righteous attempt—and all sound Protestants, except a few

Haldanes, admit this to have been a righteous one—does not decide a question of morals or of religion.

The illustration is precisely in point. Other governments may not be liable to just the same objections as was the British administration; but to others equally valid. Their oppression may be different in form—their relations to religion, and treatment of the church different, and, moreover, the mass of the people may go along with them in these things. But what then? The question is, Do they oppress knowingly and obstinately? Do they slight and dishonor religion? Do they bestow their favors upon any kind of false religion? Do they disregard God and repudiate the paramount authority of His Bible? Are they guilty of any or of all of these sins? If so, then, whether they be few or many, the friends of liberty, of religion, and of God, should withhold from them their conscientious obedience; for they are not "a terror to evil doers, and a praise to them that do well." This cannot be denied, we repeat, except upon grounds that would entirely destroy the right of civil revolution.

4. *It is affirmed that the tenor of scriptural example, and some of the teachings of Christ, are against our doctrine.* (1.) The principle examples are those of Joseph and Daniel in accepting and exercising authority in heathen kingdoms. On these we remark, that in their cases there is every reason to believe that there was no obligation incurred by either of them to conform to any immoral law, and that in their administration, the law of God was in fact made, so far as their own particular functions were concerned, the rule of their administration. They had nothing to do with any thing but the duties of their own office. Neither directly or indirectly were they required to concur in the idolatries of those nations or to sanction any acts of oppression.

These and similar cases are thus disposed of by a late writer.

Objections Answered

Any office may be held, or service engaged in, upon the three following conditions:

First, that the duties belonging to it be right in themselves.

Second, that they be regulated by a just law.

Third, that there be no other oath of office required, but faithfully to execute official duties.

Let these be the stipulations, and an office may be held under any power, however immorally constituted, without a homologation of its immorality.

JOSEPH RULING IN EGYPT

Suppose I were in Algiers, residing there at pleasure; would my accepting an office from the Dey, under the regulations now specified, say a professorship in a university instituted by him, for the instruction of youth, be a homologation of his immoral regency—naval piracy—or the blood and murder upon which his throne is erected? If there as a *slave*, would not the appointment be still more eligible? This corresponds with the situation of the captives in Babylon: it does not, therefore, follow, that holding an office necessarily supposes, either that the government be lawful; or if not, that the person holding the office is implicated in the immorality....

If it be pleaded that the monarch's will was the constitution, this, even if admitted, makes no difference. The office was either such as required allegiance to this constitution, or it did not. If the latter, it is the thing contended for, viz., that there was no immoral obligation connected with his office. If the former, he was perjured, not only by breaking it in several instances, but in taking it also, for he swore to a blank, i.e., to perform he knew not what. But there is no account of Daniel's coming under any such obligation. Indeed, it would have been inconsistent with the smiles of Heaven, which he, and others in office, evidently enjoyed.[4]

(2.) Reference is made to the language and conduct of Christ, Matthew 17:24–27; 22:21. In the former we have an account of the paying of a certain tribute, and in the latter we have the reply of Christ to an inquiry put by the Pharisees, when he says, "Render to Caesar the things that are Caesar's."

To these we reply in the words of the writer just quoted:

---

4. From *Sons of Oil* by Samuel B. Wylie, late of Philadelphia.

CHRIST AND THE ISSUE OF TAXATION

The allegation brought from Matthew 17:27, is evidently unfounded. The best commentators consider the tribute here mentioned to be temple money, the ransom of the soul spoken of, Exodus 30:12, 13. That this was the case will appear evident, first, because the piece of money found in the fish's mouth is allowed, by the best critics, to be equal in value to two half shekels, one for Christ, and the other for Peter. And, secondly, from the argument by which our Lord pleads exemption, namely, from the example of the kings of the earth. 'What thinkest thou, Simon? Of whom do the kings of the earth take custom or tribute? Of their own children, or of strangers? Peter saith unto him, Of strangers. Jesus saith unto him, Then are the children free.' Here we find, by the example of earthly kings, Christ was free. How was he free? By being the Son to the King to whom the tribute belonged. Who was this King? It could not be Caesar. Was Christ Caesar's son? No. For had he been Caesar's son, it must have been by natural generation, adoption or citizenship. None of all these was the case. And even though the last had taken place, which is the only plausible supposition, (though false,) it would not have procured this immunity, because citizenship did not exempt from tribute. But Jesus was the Son of God of heaven, that King to whom this tribute belonged; hence he says, 'notwithstanding,' that is though I am free, by the relation of Sonship, etc.

The other allegation brought from Matthew 22:21, 'Render to Caesar the things that are Caesar's,' &c., is equally unfounded. It is abundantly evident, from the passage, that the question was intended to ensnare the Lord Jesus Christ, answer as he would. It was proposed by the Herodians and Pharisees; those, votaries for Roman domination, and these, the sticklers for Jewish immunities. Had he said, 'Give it to Caesar,' the Pharisees, ever ready to accuse him, would have represented him to the people as an enemy of their ancient privileges. Had he said, 'Don't give it,' the Herodians would have represented him to Herod as an enemy to the government of Caesar. In the fifteenth verse, we are expressly told they came to him with a view to 'entangle him in his talk.' But he, 'knowing their craftiness,' split their dilemma, and left their question undecided. He, on several other occasions, thus baffled his adversaries; as in John 8:4, 12, in the case of the 'woman taken in adultery;' and in Luke 12:14, when application was made to him concerning the settlement of the earthly inheritance.

It is objected here, by some, 'that this explanation of our Savior's answer represents the Lord as shunning to declare the whole counsel of God— giving no answer in a case respecting sin and duty.' The inference is false. They were not without information on this very subject. They had the law and the prophets. The Lord Jesus Christ had given specific directions concerning the character of lawful rulers, Deuteronomy 17:15, to whom it was lawful to pay tribute for conscience' sake. But it was not information they wanted, but to ensnare him, let him answer as he would, as has already been shown. If

JESUS AND THE WOMAN CAUGHT IN ADULTERY

silence, or refusing to answer in every case, even in matters respecting sin and duty, let the design of the querist be what it will, be accounted criminal, in what point of light will the objector view the Lord Jesus Christ, when he finds him actually refusing to answer a question respecting sin and duty, in the case of his on authority? Mark 11:27, 33. 'Neither will I tell you (says he) by what authority I do these things.' It would be well if men would consider the awful consequences of some of their objections before they make them. But, supposing that Christ, in both the instances alluded to, had commanded tribute to be paid to Caesar, what does it prove? Unless he commanded it to be paid as a *tessera* of loyalty, it proves no more the morality of Caesar's right, than a minister of the gospel's advising one of his hearers to give the robber part of his property, to secure the remainder, would, that the minister consider the robber morally entitled to it.[5]

Hoadly says,

> But it is manifest that it was not his design to tell his adversaries, (whose ensnaring question was the occasion of this precept) what his opinion was concerning the rights of the emperor, but only to evade the danger of such an answer as they hoped to have extorted from him.[6]

(3.) Paul's appeal to Caesar has also been adduced as importing an acknowledgment of his right to rule. On this we use again the words of the *Sons of Oil*.

> To this I answer, an appeal to their tribunals no more involves in it a homologation of their lawful dominion, than an appeal from a murderer to a thief, who would be disposed to save one's life, would be a homologation of his living habitually in the breach of the eighth commandment. Suppose, for example, that the Allegheny mountains were infested with a baditti of robbers, whose captain retained so much humanity as to establish a law that no poor man should be robbed of more than ten dollars—you happen to be crossing the mountain—five of the gang

---

5. *Sons of Oil*, pp. 82–84.
6. Hoadly, p. 120.

approach you, and rob you of one hundred, which is nearly your all—you meet with the master of the fraternity—you know the law—and believe that he still has as much humanity remaining as will induce him to execute it. Will you appeal to him to cause your ninety dollars to be refunded, which are due to you by his law? If you do, will this implicate you in the immorality of the banditti, or be saying Amen to their unlawful practice? Certainly not. If this hold in the greater, it will surely hold in the less. If an appeal may be made to the captain of a band of robbers, without implication in his criminality, much more to these institutions, which, though wrong in some fundamentals, are yet aiming at the good of civil society.[7]

NERO CLAUDIUS CAESAR
(37–68 A.D)

---

7. *Sons of Oil*, pp. 81, 82.

5. *It is confidently asserted that the Roman Christians must have understood the Apostle as referring to the Roman government—enjoining subjection to it.* This is, perhaps, the prime objection, after all, to the views we have presented of the scope and bearing of this passage, and deserves a tolerably minute examination. And, (1.) The description here given of the magistrate does not correspond to that of the reigning Emperor of Rome, nor to the character of his administration. Nor are any so ignorant as to be without some knowledge of the character and doings of Nero Caesar—that he was a human monster; a bloody persecutor; a tyrant so remorseless that even pagan Rome ultimately dethroned and put him to death. How could it be said by Paul, speaking of such a man, "That he was a terror, not to good works, but to evil?"—"a minister of God to thee for good?"

We again quote Hoadly:

> If any should say that he speaks particularly of the Roman Emperor who, at this time, was a very bad man, I answer, if he were such a magistrate as did set himself to destroy the happiness of the people under him, and to act contrary to the end of his office, it is impossible that Paul should mean him particularly in this place. For the higher powers, v. 1, are the same with the rulers, v. 3, and whomsoever Paul intended, he declares to be, not a terror to good works, but to the evil. So that if the Roman Emperor were a terror to good works, and not to the evil, either Paul was grossly mistaken in his opinion of him, or he could not be particularly meant here. If Paul intended to press obedience to him, particularly, he manifestly doth it upon the supposition, that he was not a terror to good works, but to evil. And if this supposition be destroyed, the reasoning

SATAN IS CRUSHED BY MICHAEL THE ARCHANGEL

built upon it must fall, and all the obligation to subjection that is deduced from it.[8]

(2.) The scriptures clearly describe the Roman government as despotic, ungodly and bestial.

> After this I saw, in the night visions, and, behold, a fourth beast, dreadful and terrible, and strong exceedingly; and it had great iron teeth; it devoured and brake in pieces, and stamped the residue with

---

8. Hoadly, p. 48.

> the feet of it; and it was diverse from all beasts that were before it; and it had ten horns (Daniel 7:7).

> And I stood upon the sand of the sea, and saw a beast rise up out of the sea, having seven heads and ten horns; and upon his horns ten crowns; and upon his heads the name of blasphemy (Revelation 13:1).

All sound Protestant expositors unite in applying these prophecies to the Roman Empire. That they should be so applied ought not to be questioned. Now, is it possible that the same Spirit who dictated these prophecies, did also teach Paul to delineate this savage beast of prey, "dreadful and terrible," as a "terror to evil doers, and a praise to them that do well?" The thing is incredible. "Doth a fountain send forth, at the same hole, sweet water and bitter?" is the inquiry of an inspired writer. Does the blessed Spirit send forth teachings so diametrically opposite? We cannot believe it. He gives the true character of this huge and destroying power in the book of Daniel, as it rages among the nations—trampling and rending them, and gorging itself with their blood. Such a power He never claims as His. The passage before us cannot apply to Rome.[9]

(3.) It cannot, because one part of the mission of the gospel was and is to overthrow and utterly demolish it. For this purpose, among others, Christ reigns. This, also, was long before revealed.

> And in the days of these kings shall the God of heaven set up a kingdom which shall never be destroyed; and the kingdom shall not be left to other people, but it shall break in pieces and consume all these kingdoms (Daniel 2:44).

---

9. See Appendix D, p. 141

'These [the ten horns] shall make war with the Lamb,
and he shall overcome them' (Revelation 17:14).

But why quote? Throughout the whole prophetic scriptures—
both Old Testament and New—this great, ungodly, tyrannical,
persecuting and blasphemous power, is presented as the object of divine wrath, to be consumed, together with the "little
horn" (Daniel 8)—or the "two-horned beast" (Revelation 13)—
by the word and by the judgment of God—to be consumed
for its iniquities committed against God and his gospel. Did
the Spirit of Christ enjoin upon the Christians a conscientious
"fear," "honor," and obedience, to a system against which the
Bible teems with the weightiest denunciations?

These inquiries assume a deeper meaning and importance,
if we remember that the passage before us enjoins not mere
"submission," but a true support and cooperation—that it is
not left optional to withhold from these "powers" designated
in the text. Now, is it credible that Paul intended to teach that
Christians should incorporate with the Roman Empire? Even
the "body of the beast" is to be "given to the burning flame."
(Daniel 7:11) And again, in Revelation 13:8, it is said that "all
that dwell on earth shall worship him (the seven-headed and
ten-horned beast) whose names *are not written in the book of
life.*" We cannot conceive that the same God who moved John
thus to write, did, but a generation before, inspire Paul to command Christians to incorporate with this same beast and become constituents of his empire.

(4.) We are not without very express testimony that the
primitive Christians were not countenanced in doing—were
even forbidden to do certain acts which might be regarded as
importing an acknowledgment of the claims of Rome. "Dare
any of you," says Paul, (1 Corinthians 6:1) "having a matter

against another, go to law before the unjust and not before the saints?" It cannot be disputed that the settlement of pecuniary matters and disputes, is one of the functions of civil government. This was contemplated in its institution. And we cannot imagine how it could be wrong in the Christian to appeal for redress to any ordinance of God in reference to such matters as lie within its own province. God set up a civil government in Israel. Before its courts, Jews were to implead one another. To the civil tribunals they were to bring, as their proper place, all civil causes. When civil government is purified—and it yet will be—all such controversies will be settled by it action. Why then does Paul forbid the Corinthians making such a reference of their personal affairs to the Roman tribunals? Can it be accounted for on any other principle than this? that such proceedings would, at least, appear to involve them in an acknowledgment of their right to administer law to Christians, as being to them the ordinance of God. Moreover, he calls the Roman magistrates "the unjust." Did he, then, at one time, so speak of them, and, shortly after, urge upon Christians a conscientious subjection to their authority and maintenance of their government, inasmuch as they were a "terror to evil doers, and a praise to them that do well?" Assuredly not. In a word, Paul enjoins upon the Corinthians to withhold from the tribunals of the Roman Empire a part of that "honor" which certainly belongs to all recognized governments; and, in so doing, establishes a principle that would operate, with no little power, in keeping them and the Christians separate from the community in which they lived—that would remind them that while *in*, they were not *of*, the Roman State.

Now, much of all this that we have adduced in the last few pages, was before the minds of the Romans. They knew that Daniel had described that government as bestial—they had heard, no doubt, of the directions given to the Christians of Corinth—they understood, and to this we particularly refer, that the Roman Emperor and government were idolatrous and oppressive—that the gospel was preached, often at the hazard of life, and that its profession even was extensively discountenanced. How would they, then, understand this chapter? We put, in reply, another interrogatory.

How would the inhabitants of Papal Rome—the city itself—now understand the very same teachings? We address them:

> Brethren—be subject to the higher powers. They are the ministers of God to thee for good. They are a terror to evil doers, and a praise to them that do well. Do that which is good, and thou shalt have praise of the same.

What would they say? We can easily imagine their countenances, at first marked with some astonishment. "Can this be our government? No! it cannot. Are not our friends—the friends of the Bible—banished or executed? Are we not deprived of our liberties? Have we not seen deeds—do we not witness them almost daily—of the grossest oppression? Are not evil doers in high places? Are not the God-fearing regarded with jealousy? Is not the Bible—God's own book—a forbidden volume? Is not the gospel hated and opposed, and idolatry publicly practiced and protected? No. It cannot be that Pius IX and his ghostly government are here described, and that we are commanded, on pain of damnation, to support, fear and honor them."

To what conclusions would intelligent minds come? Why, certainly, to this, that, whatever the import of the passage, it could not apply to their governors. So would a godly Austrian—so a Hungarian—so a Spaniard—so a *slave* in the United States. Hence we add—

(5.) To apply this to the Roman government is to dishonor religion. It is time that religion—the true religion—was rid of this reproach. It is doing no little evil. Convince men that any government that happens to exist, whatever its character, is to be obeyed, honored and reverenced; we mean that the Bible enjoins this, and you have struck a very heavy blow at the Bible itself. Men—if they believe in God at all—cannot believe He is the patron of iniquity and wrong. And, hence, they will refuse to recognize the claims of any book that professes to come from God, and yet so represents him.

But of what use, then, was this passage? Why did it find a place in this epistle? Why in the volume of inspiration at all? We answer: [1.] That it was designed to show that civil government is not, as an institution, abolished by the advent of the Messiah and the setting up of his kingdom among the Gentile nations. In other words, that the ecclesiastical was not the only social power—that civil society was not to be absorbed by the church. It was important to state this distinctly; for there has ever been a tendency developed, in connection with every great religious movement, to depreciate the *institution* of magistracy—to regard it as beneath the Christian to pay any respect to political regimen, or, in any circumstances, to take a part in managing civil affairs, except so far as they may be connected with the government of the church. This spirit was, unquestionably, developed in the church at a very early period. It made its appearance during the Reformation in Germany, in Holland, and in England. It is sometimes seen in the quite intelligent now, who suppress, in their own minds, all interest in political movements, not so much from conviction respecting their practical or doctrinal corruptions, as from a mistaken notion that they are not spiritual enough at least for the devout and godly.

Every disposition of this sort is rebuked by this passage. It stands with a few parallel passages; and has stood ever, as an impregnable bulwark against such delusive notions.

[2.] It furnished then, as now, a standard by which to try existing governments. That it was not intended to induce them to "honor"—and reverence and sustain, the imperial authority of Nero, we have already endeavored to show. They could not so understand it. At first, they might be somewhat surprised—but soon—upon a little reflection, they would see that in these verses the Apostle had really furnished a very clear mirror in which they could see, by contrast, the hideous features of the "beastly" power of Rome. It is of use in this way still. The lineal descendants of the ancient Italians, who cannot discern in their own rulers, as we have seen, any traces of the beneficent power here described, may learn most important lessons. They may find that governments, whatever claim of divine right they may set up, are not above the examination of the Christian citizen—and, more than this, here are the very tests to apply.

[3.] It presented then, and does now, the specific ends which the godly should seek to attain in their reforming efforts. It has already been hinted that the word of God, the gospel of Christ, is intended to overthrow immoral and despotic power. It will do more: it will accomplish a complete reformation; and this by the instrumentality of well instructed and faithful men, who labor with an intelligent eye to a fixed and definite end. This end they find here. Not only here, for it appears elsewhere in the inspired record; but here stated with singular definiteness, distinctness and brevity. Setting this before them, the friends of Christ and of the welfare of man are engaged in no aimless work. Their toils in this department of their efforts have this as their object—the ultimate establishment of governmental authority that shall honor God and religion, shall enact just laws, protect-

ORIGEN (185–254 A.D.

ing the poor, and restraining all wrong, and that shall seek as their highest aim to advance the name and glory of Christ.

[4.] The Christians in Rome would find here ample reason for the study of quietness and patience and sedulous discharge of all the common duties of life; for here is seen, with the utmost clearness, the importance of civil society, and the imperative character of social duties. Here the fact is presented in the boldest relief, that the commission of crime, the unnecessary disturbance of the peace of the community, such conduct as denominates one a "bad citizen," whether in the narrower or the wider sense of the phrase, is deserving of "wrath"; that the practice of the Christian virtues—what these are we learn else-where—meets with commendation: is pleasing to God.

Hence, it may be added, the wise student of Romans 13:1–7, will rise from his investigations deeply impressed on the one hand with the wide departures from its high standard which have characterized and yet do characterize, the kingdoms of this world, and, of course, with a confirmed determination to refuse them his active support, but, on the other hand, with a profound and salutary conviction of the excellence of the *institution* of government, and the weighty responsibilities that rest upon the Christian as he sustains many relations to society around him. He will thus be guarded against a spirit of sedition or lawlessness, and imbued with a disposition to attend to the requirements of duty in his own particular sphere, so that while he may exemplify the faithfulness of the witness for Christ, he may still "lead a quiet and peaceable life in all godliness and honesty" (1 Timothy 2:2).

[5.] There is not wanting evidence that the primitive Christians did gather at least much of this sort of instruction from these teachings of Paul. We once more quote Hoadly:

> It is very remarkable that Origen, (the same person who challenges Celsus, that great enemy to Christians, to name any sedition, or tumult in which the Christians were concerned,) is by some alleged for this in defense of passive obedience; that he, (I say,) should mention that celebrated passage of Paul, (Romans 13:1,) upon which some have built so much, with such a remark as would incline one to think that all the primitive Christians did not see any such unlimited non-resistance in it as many have done since. The passage I mean is towards the end of his eighth book against Celsus, where he takes occasion to cite this place of Paul, to show the adversaries of

Christianity what notions Christians had concerning princes, and the subjection due to them. But he immediately adds that there were many questions and disputations about the meaning of this place of Scripture, arising from the consideration of the cruelty and tyranny of many princes; and that upon that account he would not at present undertake to give an exact account of it. From whence I think it manifest, not only that many of the first Christians doubted whether the subjection preached by Paul was due, in point of conscience, to tyrants and oppressors; but also that Origen himself, when he wrote this, did not believe it to be so. For if he did, he had now the fairest occasion for declaring it; and he could not more effectually have defended the Christians from the objections now before him, than by saying so.[10]

This passage was far from useless to the Romans, though it did not teach them conscientious obedience to a rampant savage power. It taught them better things, more becoming Christians. To us it brings the same lessons.

6. It may be objected that *to withhold allegiance from ungodly governments is not practicable—that lands must be held—taxes paid—the laws appealed to for redress.* We reply,

(1.) That property is not held of the state. The state—the nation—does not give the title. Or if it be in any case original proprietor, the purchase of land from the state no more implies a recognition of its other claims than the purchase of property from an individual recognizes all his acts, and endorses his character.

(2.) Taxes may be paid, either on business principles merely, for work done, or for the reason that if they be not paid, they will be *taken.* Circumstances may occur making it an imperative

---

10. Hoadly, p. 139

duty to refuse the payment of taxes at all hazards, but ordinarily this would be unwise because ineffectual, and would answer no end that cannot, at least as well, be otherwise obtained.

(3.) The courts may be appealed to on principles already stated and vindicated.[11]

(4.) We reply, in general, to every objection of this sort, that we must distinguish between things that belong merely to matters of social neighborhood and arrangement, and things governmental; that there is a vast difference between men's availing themselves merely of natural rights, and taking an active and, of course, voluntary part in affairs of state. And, finally, that all these acts, which are comprehended in this class of objections, are acts which aliens may do, and privileges used such as aliens enjoy, and yet no one imagines that the alien becomes, by such acts as buying lands, etc., a corporate member of the body politic.

Our principle will stand the most rigid investigation—it demands the closest examination. For it is a matter of no small moment to ascertain well that we do not so identify ourselves with institutions that dishonor God and oppress man, as to involve ourselves in their guilt and punishment, or weaken our own hands in the efforts we may be disposed to make for their reformation.

---

11. See page 112

Conclusion

And, 1. *There is no such sacredness about civil governments as to exempt them from the closest scrutiny in their constitution and workings.* The time was when it would have been necessary to dwell largely upon this statement. The occupants of power are always disposed to claim an uninquiring recognition, as well as an unresisting obedience Kings and emperors have been addressed by the title of "sacred majesty." They have claimed a "divine right" to reign. They are kings "by the grace of God." They are to rule and the people to submit, pay taxes, and bear all the burdens. This was once the theory. Some changes have, indeed, passed over society in many Christian countries. Men do not now yield so readily a blind and superstitious obedience. But, after all, the principle is not yet fully recognized that, like everything else in human hands, the affairs of government are, in every aspect, opened to be questioned and tried. Even in this land, with all its licentiousness of opinion and even contempt of authority, there is yet not a little of the old leaven. Not a few still appear to regard the constitution, and even some enactments, and these the worst of them, as possessing a sort of extraordinary sacredness.

For all this there is no reason. The Church is, surely, as sacred as the state, and yet what friend of religious liberty denies the right of the Lord's freeman to bring her claims to the proof—to try her proceedings? It is one of the peculiarities of the great Apostasy, to demand an uninquiring subjugation of the understanding and conscience to its arrogant demand of implicit recognition and obedience. The faithful repudiate the claim. They have ever insisted that to admit it would be treason against Christ.

Nor in divesting government of *this kind* of sacredness do we furnish any opening for either licentiousness or sedition. The standard—the chief standard—of judgment here, as in all other matters where morals are concerned, is the Word of God. We do not reject reason altogether. But reason itself must be proved by the same word. And it has been previously observed that when the Holy Scriptures are conscientiously regarded and justly applied, the result will be, on the one hand, the rejection of what God does not approve, and on the other hand, the intelligent and hearty subjection of the whole man to what accords with the divine will. And can it be considered as anything short of an infidel contempt of the Bible to assert that to use it for this purpose is either wrong or dangerous to the peace and order of society?

2. *Tried by this supreme rule, the government of this land cannot claim conscientious obedience.* It has, indeed, been set up by the action, and, of course, exists by the voice of the majority of the people. But this is not the only test. The people may be wrong now, as well as of old, when the ten tribes "set up kings, but not by" God, "and princes, and he Knew [approved] it not" (Hosea 7:3, 4). That this has been done in these states is evident because the paramount authority of the Most High, speaking in his word, is not recognized in the constitution—the fundamental law of the general government; because Christ is not, in any sense, acknowledged in his character as "Prince of the kings of

128

the earth" (Revelation 1:3), because the Bible is not received as law, obligatory and supreme; because no barrier has been enacted against the induction of God's enemies into places of power—of trust; because the same securities are thrown around the idolatries of Popery, as around the practice and observances of the true religion; because oppression is sanctioned, and the oppressor protected in the enjoyment of his despotic and unfounded claim. In this last we refer, of course, to slavery, which is numbered among the "institutions" of nearly one-half of the states, and the constitution gives the same protection to this institution as to any others. It does more. It provides specific and peculiar means for the arrest of the fugitive; or, perhaps, more accurately, it contains provisions, which may be made, and have been, the basis of distinct legislation on this subject.[1]

Now, let it be remembered, that to constitute an oppressive and tyrannical government, it is not requisite that the subjects of the violence and wrong be white men: it is enough if they be men—nor that they be the majority, kept under by a well situated and armed minority, as in Italy or Austria. Any institutions are chargeable with the sin and *crime* of despotism, that willfully deprive any class of their citizens of their natural rights, or sanction it when done. This is the case here. The constitution treats as outcasts from its pale a large proportion of the inhabitants of the country, more than three millions out of twenty-four. Hence, it is not only wrong and sinful to swear to maintain the constitution: we go farther, and affirm that such a government is not to be "honored" as God's moral ordinance; it is not,—as it respects a host within its limits, and these belonging to that very class, the poor and needy, for whose protection civil government was eminently designed—a "minister of God for good," but a minister of *evil.*

---

1. See Appendix E, p. 143

To such a government the apostle has here no reference in his injunctions of obedience. It does not possess the features here required. It possesses some that are here, by implication, strongly condemned.

We are aware that it is no easy task to persuade men—even intelligent men—that this is a matter in which they have a deep, personal, and responsible interest. The evil of corrupt government is one so nearly universal and of so long standing—the notion is so prevalent that if there is anything wrong, it is not *their* concern; and the obstacles are often so many and so great in the way of a complete withdrawing from an active share in affairs of state; and, finally, it is so easy to lull the conscience by the delusive idea that the best way to reform a government is first to swear to support it, and to take a part in its operations. In view of all these considerations, it is a matter of labor and of effort, and cannot be accomplished unless the Spirit of God imparts clear and spiritual vision, and gives a decided and resolute will.[2]

3. *Such as do take this step are called to a position of peculiar difficulty.* On the one hand they are to watch against doing anything really inconsistent with the place which they have deliberately occupied—apart from the governmental machinery; at the same time testifying with candor and faithfulness against existing wrong—and yet, on the other hand, they need to be equally watchful lest they be tempted to despise even the institution of government, become regardless of the welfare of the land, or in any way disorderly in their deportment. It is especially required of them that "they follow every good work," and thus by a pure and peaceable behavior as individual, and by the exemplariness of their deportment in social life, commend to all men the excellence of a full and faithful profession

---

2. See Appendix C, p. 137

of the name of Christ, or at least, that "by well doing, they may put to silence the ignorance of foolish men."

4. *The doctrines of this passage and the collateral principles to which we have referred, will certainly yet prevail on earth.* The very fact that Paul was inspired of God to give such a view of civil authority is a guarantee that it shall yet receive a just exemplification. However this may be, other scriptures are more explicit.

> The kingdom and dominion, and the greatness of the kingdom under the whole heaven, shall be given to the saints of the Most High (Daniel 7:27).

> The kings of Tarshish and of the isles shall bring presents: the kings of Sheba and Seba shall offer gifts. Yea, all kings shall fall down before him; all nations shall serve him. For he shall deliver the needy when he crieth; the poor also, and him that hath no helper. He shall spare the poor and needy, and shall save the souls of the needy. He shall redeem their souls from deceit and violence: and precious shall their blood be in his sight (Psalm 72:10–14).

> And kings shall be thy nursing fathers, and their queens thy nursing mothers (Isaiah 49:23).

> Blessed and holy is he that hath part in the first resurrection: on such the second death hath no power, but they shall be priests of God and of Christ, and shall reign with him a thousand years (Revelation 20:6).

The apostle John thus describes the ultimate issue of the vast changes in reference to things religious, political, and social, in the following most expressive and emphatic language:

The kingdoms of this world are become the kingdoms of our Lord and of his Christ, and he shall reign forever and ever (Revelation 11:15).

Even so come, Lord Jesus.

Appendix A

Pg. 10

The word "εξουσια" has been a good deal insisted upon as denoting a power lawful before God. It is derived from a verb "εξεστι"—"it is lawful." Still, we would not insist upon this so far as to lay any great stress upon it in argument. It is not necessary to do so; and, moreover, the term is used in Revelation 13:3, to express the "authority" of the beast of the sea.

Appendix B

Pg. 12

On the word "υπερεχουσαις" more stress may be, perhaps, laid. The following is from a lecture on the Revelation, by Murray, of Newcastle, England:

> There is a passage, which has been much improved by those that imagine that believers of the Gospel are, by the Apostle, enjoined to yield a passive obedience, and that is in Romans 13:1, which version reads, 'Let every soul be subject to the higher powers,' &c., to the beginning of the seventh verse. With all due respect to our translators, and other learned men, I will affirm that this is rather a paraphrase of the translators, than a translation of the text. From the very genius of the Greek language, it is manifest that εξουσιαις υπερεχουσαις do not signify all sorts of authority, but only such as protect men in the enjoyment of their just rights and privileges; and these words ought to be read literally, *protecting authorities*, or *excellent authorities*. Εξουσια in its first signification, signifies *just and lawful power or authority*, and can never be applied to tyrants and oppressors without abuse: υπερεχω signifies to protect, or to be eminent, and is here understood in that sense, as in other Greek authors. Homer makes

use of *this* word in *this sense*, when he describes Agamemnon addressing the Greeks, when the Trojans were advancing against them, (*Illiad*. iv. l. 249) —'Will ye tarry,' says he, 'till the Trojans advance, to know whether Jupiter will protect you?' Οφρα ιδητ αικ υμιν υπερσχη χειρα Κρονιων. This Apostle makes use of this word, (Philippians 4:7) to point out the excellency of the peace of God. Και ειρηνη του Θεου η υπερεχουσα παντα νουν; *and the peace of 'God which, passeth all understanding, shall keep your hearts.'* This same Apostle, in the second chapter of this Epistle, makes use of the same word to signify excellency, or what is more excellent, or better; αλληλους ηγουμεντας υπερεχοντας '*let each esteem others better than themselves.*' It does not appear from this passage that there is any command to be subject to any powers, except such as excel, and protect their subjects.

Appendix C

Pg. 39, 130

M urray takes the same view that we have done of this passage. He says:—

> But let us read the whole paragraph, without any paraphrase in the translation, and see how it will prove non-resistance.
>
> Let every soul be subordinate to the authorities protecting them; for it is not authority if not from God. But these that are authorities under God, are appointed. Therefore, he that resisteth the authority resisteth the appointment of God, and they that resist shall receive judgment to themselves. For rulers are not a terror of good works, but of evil. Will you not fear authority? do good, and you shall have praise from it; for he is the servant of God for good. But if you do evil, fear, for he beareth not the sword in vain; for he is the servant of God, a revenger for wrath to him that doeth evil. Therefore, it is necessary to obey, not only for *wrath*, but for *conscience's* sake. For this cause pay you tribute also, for they are the servants of God, waiting continually for this very thing. Render therefore to all their due; tribute to whom tribute, custom to whom custom, fear to whom fear, honor to whom honor.

Can any words make the subject more plain, that it is the appointment of God, and the ruler answering the character here given him, that lays the obligation upon Christians to obey him? If the people who bring Romans 13:1 as a proof of mere passive obedience to all sorts of superiors, will please to read the text carefully, the arguments they use will vanish, whether they will or not. It is plain to a demonstration that as the Apostle does not here appoint any particular form of government, so he says nothing of the present rulers, but recommends subjection to governors in general; and that from the consideration of the Divine institution of their office, and the advantage thereof to mankind, when rightly administered. To resist such governors as answer the end of their office, and the Apostle's representation is, no doubt, a great crime, and deserves a proportionable punishment, called here κριμα (*judgment,*) both in this life, and that which is to come. But the resisting of tyranny and tyrants falls not under the sentence of the Apostle. The text says nothing to the case of tyrants, but really excludes them as being another sort of creatures from what he describes, and the very reverse of that character which he gives the minister of God, to whom he requires subjection.

They are not at all authorities of God, according to the Apostle, if they are a terror to good works, and a praise to evil; for the authorities appointed by God are appointed for this end. And the authority that does not answer this end is not an authority that it is lawful to obey. In such a case, the threatening should be read backwards, namely, 'he that resisteth not the power shall receive (κριμα) *judgment.*' If any person were to read a Greek classic as these advocates for passive obedience read the New

Testament, they would be posted up as enemies to true literature and common sense, by all the literati in the three kingdoms. The Apostles have nowhere affirmed, that Christians, at the pleasure of despots, were to surrender their liberties more than others, who were fellow citizens with them, in the same country. If both the rulers and the rest of the subjects differ with them, they have no other shift but to remonstrate against their oppression, suffer, or forsake their country.

Milton says:

The words immediately after make it as clear as the sun, that the Apostle speaks only of a lawful power; for he gives us in them a definition of magistrates, and thereby explains to us who are the persons thus authorized, and upon what account we are to yield obedience, lest we should be apt to mistake, and ground extravagant notions upon hid discourse. *'Magistrates,'* says he, *'are not a terror to good works, but to evil. Wilt thou, then, not be afraid of the power? Do that which is good, and thou shalt have praise of the same; for he is the minister of God to thee for good: he beareth not the sword in vain; for he is the minister of God, a revenger, to execute wrath upon him that doeth evil.'* What honest man would not willingly submit to such a magistracy as is here described, and that not only to avoid wrath, and for fear of punishment, but *for conscience's sake?* Whatever power enables a man, or whatsoever magistrate takes upon him to act contrary to what Paul makes the duty of those that are in authority, neither is that power nor that magistrate ordained of God; and, consequently, to such a magistrate no subjection is commanded, nor is any due; nor are the people forbidden to resist such authority; for in so doing, they do not resist the power nor the magistracy, as they are here excellently well described; but they resist a robber, a tyrant, an enemy, who, if he may notwithstanding, in some sense, be called a magistrate upon this account only, because he has power in his hands—by the same reason, the devil may be called a magistrate.

Appendix D

Pg. 116

As to the true origin of the Roman power, it is stated in Revelation 13:5,

> And the dragon gave him his power and state and great authority.

On this *Dr. Junkin* says:

> Now the source of this power is pointed out. The dragon gave it to him: Diabolus formed this city and government for himself.

Dr. Scott says:

> The dragon may here mean either the devil, or the *devil's vicegerent*, the idolatrous Roman Empire. — So that when another idolatrous persecuting power had succeeded to that of the heathen emperors, then 'the dragon' had transferred his dominion to 'the beast,' or the devil had appointed another vicegerent, and all the world knows that this occurred to the history of the Roman Empire, Pagan and Papal.

Dr. Junkin adds:

The scripture account of absolute despotism (he might have said of all godless and Christless power,) is, that Satan gave it, and the *blasphemous slander of God* is the argument by which the doctrine of legitimacy is sustained from the Bible. 'Our power is of God.' 'The powers that be are ordained of God,' —therefore iron-handed despotism is a divine institution. This is the conclusion of its friends, but the word of truth proclaims it to be from below. The same kind of logic will prove the devil's own usurpation to be right and proper ... The fallacy lies here in a false assumption. Paul says, 'The powers that be, εχουσιαι, that is, *civil government*, is an ordinance of God; and the assumption is that it means arbitrary power —might without right. This is the logic by which Diabolus has blasphemed the Creator for a score of centuries. (See *Lectures on Revelation*, pp 209, 210).

Appendix E

Pg. 129

The arrogance of the Papists, both in England and in this country, is already beginning to awaken doubts whether after all it is safe to admit the votaries of superstition, and the subjects of such a spiritual despotism, to the full enjoyment of political rights among a Protestant people. God will yet avenge, and by the Papists themselves, as his instruments, nations that have not only given equal honor and protection to Christ's church and her anti-Christian counterfeit, but have boasted of this as a suitable display of liberality.

Dr. Junkin says:

> The grand defect in the bond of our national union is the absence of the recognition of God as the Governor of this world. We have omitted —may it not be said, refused? —to own Him whose head wears many crowns, as having any right of dominion over us. The constitution of the United States contains no express recognition of the being of a God; much less an acknowledgment that *The Word of God* sways the scepter of universal dominion. This is our grand national sin of omission. This gives the infidel occasion to glory, and has no small influence in fostering infidelity in affairs of state, and among

political men. That the nation will be blessed with peace and prosperity continuously, until this defect be remedied, no Christian philosopher expects. For this national insult, the Governor of the universe will lift again and again his rod of iron over our heads, until we be affrighted, and give this glory to his name. (*Lectures on Revelation*, pp 280-1).

Appendix F

AN ESSAY ON SUBMISSION TO THE
POWERS THAT BE

Does the law of God require of Christians a conscientious submission to all existing governments? Or are we at liberty, and required to make preliminary inquiries respecting the moral character of a government previously to our yielding such a submission to its commands? We do not now speak of active support, as by oaths of allegiance, or by taking part in the administration. Our inquiry relates to submission. Nor do we discuss the propriety of obeying laws that contravene God's law. On this point the Christian has explicit and unmistakable direction. He is to "obey God rather than man." Nor do we treat of a forced conformity to civil regulations and enactments, in themselves not unlawful. This is certainly allowable. It is submission for "wrath's sake" (Rom. 13:5). We are considering something different from any of these, *viz.,* whether it is a Christian duty to acknowledge conscientiously, and as God's ordinance, *any* existing government, whatever its moral character. To this we will attempt to furnish an answer in the course of the examination of the following passage. It will be found in 1 Peter 2:13–16: *"Submit yourselves to every ordinance of man for the Lord's sake: whether it be to the king, as supreme; or unto governors, as unto them that are sent by him for the punishment of evil-doers, and for the praise of them that do well. For so is the will of God, that with well-doing ye may put to silence the ignorance of foolish men: as free, and not using your liberty for a cloak of maliciousness, but as the servants of God."*

On this, we remark—

I. That the terms employed here denote civil authorities, whatever the titles of their magistrates, higher and subordinate. From the use, in this passage, and elsewhere in Scripture, of the title "king," to denote civil powers, we are not to infer, as some have done, that the Scriptures sanction, much less enjoin, monarchical government, as alone agreeable to God's ordinance of magistracy. And, first, 1. If monarchs *alone* are meant here, *inferior* magistrates must be called governors, for so they are styled in the text. 2. The magistrates of ancient Israel were called in different periods by different names, and the government itself was far from having always the same form. For four hundred years after their settlement in the land of Canaan, they had no regular and unbroken succession of chief magistrates. Such as they had, and their administrations embraced the largest part of the four hundred years, they were styled "judges." The highest authorities in the various tribes were even less distinctly designated. 3. So far from enjoining monarchical, the Scriptures favor a republican or representative form of government. The example of Israel, just referred to, is exactly in point. Among that people, many of their ordinary magistrates were evidently elective. "Choose ye out from among you," says Moses to the twelve tribes; and this was certainly the principle of the political arrangements of Moses: a principle but little interfered with upon the introduction of the monarchical form at a subsequent period. Hence, though God

146

had designated the person in whose hands the royal power was to be lodged,—the voice of the people was not disregarded. Witness the election of Saul, and of David, and the supplications presented by the people to Rehoboam when the people came to "Shechem to make him king" (1 Kings 12:1). The truth is, 4. That the name of the chief magistrate, and even the particular form, as it relates to distribution of powers, and the whole subject of checks and balances, is a matter, in itself, of indifference. The grand requisite, as we shall show presently, is, that in all these matters there be a constant regard in every element and principle to bring them into accordance with the moral law of God. This appears in the passage, for—

II. Civil government is here described as an "ordinance of man": "submit yourselves to every ordinance of man." The term "ordinance" is not used here in the same sense which we now frequently put upon it. In common parlance a civil "ordinance" is a municipal regulation,—a law ordained by a town council, or some peculiar enactment of the supreme authority. Here, it signifies the system of government set up and in operation. Hence, it follows, "to the king as supreme," etc. But how is government an "ordinance of man"? Does it mean that civil government is a mere human device, that it has no higher origin than the voice of the nation? That it is a mere voluntary association which men may form or not, or that when formed it may be modeled as men please, irrespective of the claims of the Most High? Certainly not: "the powers that be are ordained of God,"—Romans 13:1,—a fact which we may gather from the very constitution of man as a social being,—made for society, for co-operation with his fellows. Civil government has a higher origin than mere human ingenuity: God is its author. He has defined its ends, its duties, and the principles of its administration. He has even determined the class of men who should alone be the depositories of civil authority: "able men, men that fear God, men of truth, and hating covetousness." How, then, is civil government an "ordinance of man"?

1. It is so called from the fact that human instrumentality is concerned in making its arrangements. Observe, not merely in giving it being, but in establishing the specific and peculiar terms of its constitution. This will appear more clearly in a literal rendering of the original words—πασῃ ανθρωπινη κτισει—"every human creation" (1 Peter 2:13). As we have already intimated, civil government is an ordinance of God, but not in such a sense as to preclude the exercise of human wisdom in what relates to its form, its various departments, its checks and balances. And hence, forms of government, in some respects very different, have existed with divine approbation. During the period of the Judges, Israel was a confederated republic. It was afterwards a limited, and, with certain reservations, an hereditary monarchy. In both these periods, however, the nation was in avowed subjection to the Most High, and its affairs were managed with divine approbation—in the spirit of the love of God, and with avowed subjection to its authority; the rights and liberties of all the people and the interest of religion being properly guarded and maintained. In this respect, there is a wide difference between civil and ecclesiastical government. The latter is, in every particular, completely arranged by Jesus Christ: the Bible contains the church's constitution. Everything relating to the officers of the church, their duties, and their powers, is fully set forth in the Scriptures. To these nothing can be added; from them nothing taken. Our business—and our only business—is to ascertain and carry out the divine will. Hence, ecclesiastical government is never denominated, as that of the state is, an "ordinance of man." But this is not all.

2. Government is a human creation, inasmuch as the constituted civil authorities are left to the exercise of a wise discretion in the enactment and rescinding of laws, as demanded by emergent circumstances. For example, in regulating commerce, the currency, taxation, and, to some extent, even what relates to education and police, states are left free to choose that plan which the times and the existing state of things render advisable. True, all civil enactments are to be brought to scriptural test—none of these must run counter to the moral law—and in some departments, as in relation to marriage, to the penalties of gross crimes, to the vindication of the Sabbath, to the support of religion—the state is directly bound by the precepts and directions of the revealed will of God. Still, there remains a wide margin. In this, again, differing from the church—all whose laws, as well as constitutional privileges, are embodied in the Scriptures, our sole business being to discover and apply them.

Hence, in perfect consistency with the principle that civil government is an "ordinance of God," it is here styled "an ordinance of man"; and we add, that in this title we find no indistinct intimation that lawful civil authority is not—cannot be—founded in the sword, nor in any absolute scheme of hereditary descent, nor in anything else which stifles the popular will.

III. This passage describes, and requires submission to, a righteous civil government. And,

1. The magistrates here spoken of are "sent" of God: "as unto them that are sent by him." But what means this term? Are we to apply it to any existing government? Are we to suppose that, irrespective of the origin of their power, or its nature, or the spirit in which it is exercised, all civil rulers that happen to occupy the seat of power are to be honored with conscientious allegiance? Certainly not. For—(1.) There have

been civil rulers, of whom God declared, in the most express terms, that He had not sent them. We refer to the kings of the ten tribes after they became an independent kingdom: "They have set up kings, but not by me; they have made princes, and I knew it not" (Hosea 8:4). Can language be more explicit? "Not by me; they have made princes." Yet this was an existing government; and, still more—and to this we ask particular attention—it was a popular government, having had its origin in a great national revolution, exercised and upheld by the voice of the people. The kings of Israel, in other words, were no usurpers; they swayed no scepter gained by conquest and blood. Yet even of these God said they were set up "not by Him," He "knew it not." The assent of the people they had, but God did not acknowledge nor recognize them. Surely, it would have been no "damnable" sin for a fearer of God to withhold from such kings conscientious submission; to such no allegiance could be due "for the Lord's sake." (2.) We have declarations equally explicit in relation to the existing idolatrous, tyrannical authorities of the old world. We refer to the language of prophecy, which denominates them as "beastly" in their origin and character, and blasphemous in their pretensions, and denounces them as doomed of God. "I saw," says Daniel, (chap. 7), "and, behold, the four winds of heaven strove upon the great sea, and four great beasts came up from the sea." The last of these—the fourth beast—was "dreadful and terrible, and strong exceedingly, and it had great iron teeth: it devoured and brake in pieces, and stamped the residue with its feet." And so John writes, "And I stood upon the sand of the sea, and saw a beast rise up out of the sea, having seven heads and ten horns, and upon his heads ten crowns, and upon his heads the name of blasphemy" (Rev. 13:1). All intelligent Protestants apply these symbolic representations to the divided Roman Empire—the existing anti-Christian thrones of Europe.[1] Did God send them? No. For even still more expressly as to their origin, John says—"And the dragon"—the devil—"gave him his power, and seat, and great authority." Can anything be clearer? How could this beast—these kings—claim conscientious submission? The devil—not God—gave them their power: a fact written as clear as the sun in the heavens upon their constitution and administration. The former, adverse to the rights of the people—the latter, directed not to the advancement of God's glory, and the interests of morality and religion, but in diametrical opposition to all these. God sends them! Yes. As he sends tempests and plagues, to scourge the nations for their sins. As he raised up Pharaoh, to show in these last times his power in their utter and signal ruin. (3.) It cannot be that God, in any such way, sends immoral powers, for then the only inquiry would be, Does a government exist? Has it the requisite vigor and resources to compel obedience to its decrees? Behind this, we could not—dare not go. Every usurper, every tyrant, every Nero, Caligula, Heliogabalus, or Borgia, might justly demand conscientious allegiance as God's minister! Do the advocates of existing powers, as God's ordinance, admit this? No. They fall back from their own argument—they insist upon some attributes as essential to a right to reign. We live in the age of revolutions. The world will not hear even the enunciation of the doctrine of passive obedience. The nations have risen, and are still rising, to demand, at least some, credentials of these pretended vicegerents of the Almighty. But, are they not powers?—are they not "powers that be"? How, then, except on our principle, can we go behind this fact, and investigate the validity of their commission? We affirm, on no other.

---

1. The vision of the "beast coming up out of the sea, having ten horns and seven heads" is most likely a reference to the Roman Empire of the first century.

Who, then, are "sent" of God? We answer, those who come bearing the law, and exhibiting, in measure, the image of God. Those who, honoring God, and seeking to accomplish the ends of his moral ordinance of magistracy, do really sustain the character, as they perform the duties of his ministers. To no others are we called upon, in God's name, and for his sake, to yield a conscientious submission.

2. The passage expressly defines them as righteous—(Rom. 13:4)—"As unto governors, as unto them that are sent by him for the punishment of evil-doers, and for the praise of them that do well." That this language defines a righteous administration of justice between man and man as an indispensable feature of civil government, without which it would have no validity—no claims upon our allegiance—is scarcely disputable. Few will be even disposed to deny this, at least in this land. For, whatever the abettors of a "divine right to rule wrong" may affirm, it is here universally acknowledged, (we go farther, maintained), that tyrants have no claim upon the conscientious submission of their subjects: that, instead, it is even a duty to throw off the yoke the very first opportunity. The contrary doctrine would involve the notion—reproachful to the Almighty—that He not merely recognizes the proud and hard-hearted despot as His vicegerent, but obliges the wretched victims of his power to look up to him with reverence as God's minister to him for good.

But, is this all? Is it enough to characterize a government as "sent" of God "for the punishment of the evil-doers, and for the praise of them that do well," that common justice be dispensed, the lawless and the turbulent restrained, and the rights of the peaceable guarded? Certainly not. Are none, in the sight of God's law—we speak of it as revealed as the law of society—are none "evil-doers" but rioters and robbers, disturbers of the public peace; and invaders of private rights? And are we to limit the phrase, "such as do well," to those who pay due regard to the common welfare, and to the rights of their fellow citizens? By no means. Wrong-doing and well-doing are both to be measured by the divine law—not merely its second, but its first table. He does wrong who dishonors God, and blasphemes his name, and profanes his Sabbath,—he does well, in a high sense, who does the opposite of all these. We might rest our argument on this point with a fair interpretation of the phrases themselves—evil and well-doing—but we have additional evidence. God so explained it in the code which he prepared for ancient Israel. The book of Revelation exhibits the same principle in its denunciation of civil government—not as tyrannical merely, but as impious; and finally, we may appeal to the common opinion of all nations—pagan and Christian, ancient and modern. For where is the nation which has taken no account—we except revolutionary France for a very short time—of such crimes as open blasphemy?

If this be granted, our principle is established. The government that claims the conscientious submission of the faithful, must be, in the sense in which we have now explained it, as well as in the former, a restraint upon evil doers, and a praise to them that do well. And why not? We admit, as we have already said, that a government that tramples upon human rights is not to be acknowledged as the minister of God. How, then, we ask, can a government be so acknowledged which puts no restraint upon the open enemies of the Most High, pays no regard to the prerogatives of Christ, and throws open its honors, and thus gives "power" to the avowed despisers of his law? Is this to answer the ends of a divine ordinance? Surely the rights of God and of Christ are not less worthy of recognition than human rights. To permit, and especially to patronize their violation is no less a crime than to refuse to the citizens of the commonwealth protection of life or property.

Now observe, all agree,—with the few exceptions already referred to,—that there are limits to the duty of submission, that at least the rights of man must not be seriously infringed. Some would, however, stop at this point. They would be satisfied with the very narrrowest sense that the terms will possibly bear. We make no such restrictions. We interpret them in light of Scripture, and of the entire history of our race, so far as it contains examples worthy of being followed. Without hesitation, we repeat our assertion that the passage enjoins conscientious submission to such a government, and to such a one only, as vindicates not merely human rights, but the rights of God,—of Him who is "King of kings and Lord of lords."

3. The fact that civil government is a divine ordinance demands this interpretation. As we have already said, provision has been made in the very constitution of human nature for the existence of civil institutions among men. And the language of Romans 13:1, is express to the point that civil government is, not a mere contrivance of men, a matter of expedience or necessity,—but an ordinance of God. "The powers that be are ordained of God." "He," the ruler, "is the minister of God to thee for good." But what does this ordinance comprehend? Does it embrace no more that the affixing of a divine sanction to the exercise of such authority among men as is denominated civil?—leaving everything relating to its ends, its limits, its exercise, completely independent of God's will and direction? Certainly not. A divine ordinance is something. God's minister has something to do in that character. And whatever government is, it must be moral—for God is holy and good. Whatever his servant has to do, he must, in doing it, bear the image of God for whom he acts. It is monstrous even to imag-

ine that the Most High has impressed his sanction upon every kind of human authority, however immoral, profane, blasphemous, requiring of the unhappy and tempted subject of such dominion, not merely a peaceful subjection to irresistible power, but a conscientious reverence of its officers and agents, as his ministers. We are not left to adopt any such revolting conclusion. The scriptures are plain. They define, as we have already remarked, the ends of civil authority,—the good of society, and God's glory; they fix the character of its officers— able men (Exodus 18:21); just men, "He that ruleth over men must be just, ruling in the fear of God" (2 Kings 23:3). They prescribe many of its laws, and enjoin upon it special duties. Now, we repeat, every ordinance of God, in its institution, is like himself, and only as it bears his image in its constitution and administration, can it possibly be required of us to yield it that high regard, and hearty acquiescence, and conscientious obedience, which is due to those to whom so high and important trusts are committed.

But, it will be said, the government then existing, which claimed the submission of Christians,—the Roman,—certainly did not possess the character of a righteous government, as we have defined it,—did not acknowledge Christ—nor regard his law. The fact is admitted, the conclusion is denied. Because, (1.) This government was one of conquest, so far as related to the provinces in which the Christians resided, whom Peter addresses, and even in Rome itself, was a military and not a popular government, and, hence, on the principles of objectors themselves, could not claim a conscientious allegiance: in other words, it was a government which might lawfully have been thrown off, even by a violent revolution. The advocates of passive obedience, and non-resistance, are constant—no others are, in adducing this objection. It strikes at the fundamental, and, in this country, generally admitted doctrine, that a mere government of force cannot claim to be God's ordinance,—cannot demand conscientious allegiance, but may be resisted, overturned, and another substituted in its stead. (2.) Intelligent Christians knew, as they know now, that this government had been denounced by the Spirit of God as the enemy of the kingdom of Christ. They understood the prophecies of Daniel, to which we have already referred, and could have had no difficulty in applying them to a government with whose history they were familiar, as one of destruction,—of trampling down and breaking in pieces. Nor, (3.) does our view involve the conclusion that these directions were of no use to the churches. This passage was designed, and would have this effect, to arrest any tendency on the part of Christians to reject entirely the ordinance of civil government; to meet the case of a class of persons which began to make their appearance at this early age, as we learn from Peter's Second Epistle to these churches, as they have often since, who rejected the ordinance of civil government altogether,—true anti-government men,—holding it to be inconsistent with Christianity, under any circumstances, to have to do with civil power. Moreover, the Scriptures were intended to be a complete rule in every age and such passages as the one before us, would point out to the faithful one grand object at which they should aim—the reformation of national organizations until they should be brought into conformity with the characteristics embodied summarily, but distinctly, in these passages themselves. These admonitions, then, were far from being useless or inapplicable, at the time, and are of immense use now. Indeed, the very fact that such directions were needed at that time, is no inconsiderable argument in favor of our view. For how could the idea have originated that Christians were adverse to civil authority, unless from the perversion of the apostolic teachings in regard to the unholy nature and unchristian character of existing institutions?

Our interpretation must stand. The passage teaches the duty of acknowledging a righteous civil government, and no other. It makes this an essential characteristic. And that, as much when the government is of popular origin, as under any other circumstances. Even of such a government, if it had this attribute, God says, as he said of the popular government of the ten tribes, "They have set up kings, but not by me; they have made princes, and I knew it not."

4. To a righteous government hearty allegiance is imperatively required. "Submit yourselves therefore." There are two kinds of submission to civil authority. One is forced—for "wrath's sake": the other is that to which we have so often alluded, a sincere, cheerful subjection—for "conscience sake," for "the Lord's sake." As to the former, circumstances may render it expedient, and even dutiful. It may be expedient, from regard to a man's personal safety,—like the submission of the peaceable inhabitant to the unjust exactions of an invading host, pouring into his country with irresistible might; or, more nearly, like the peaceable subjection of the slave to the unjust and sinful claims of his pretended owner. A subjection based upon no higher principle than the impossibility of successful resistance, and the fear of making things worse by attempting the use of violent means of relief. On these grounds, submission for wrath's sake may be expedient, and even in a sense, dutiful. Still more, the Christian regards the peace of society—he knows that the reformation of the government is a work of time and of Christian effort—he has, as a willing subject of Christ's government, a high regard for the welfare of the body politic, and is thankful for every law, and every act of administration that accords with the divine will, and

thus tends to promote the object of the ordinance of magistracy—and, besides, is careful that no just reproach shall fall, through any act of his, upon the pure and peaceful character of the gospel of Christ, and cherishes, with habitual concern, the honor of his exalted Prince and Savior. On these grounds, the intelligent Christian demeans himself quietly and honestly in all godliness, so long as his privileges and those of his fellow-Christians, and the community, are not interfered with, whatever the moral character of the government. And thus, as a matter of duty, and we may even say for "conscience sake," not as regarding the existing authorities as God's ministers, but as for other and higher reasons.

God's ordinance, however, requires more than this. It demands, as we have all along suggested, a hearty and cheerful recognition of its being and its authority, and a ready submission to its enactments, as bearing the stamp and impress of God's institution. Such a government and such officers, the Christian will honor, support, maintain and defend. This is the submission enjoined in the passage before us: "Submit, for the Lord's sake," "for so is the will of God." Such a submission as the godly Israelites gave to the Mosaic institutions, and the officers by whom they were administered—to the authority of David, and his godly successors. Such a submission as the saints will yield to the governments of the earth at that time when "the kingdoms of this world are become the kingdoms of our Lord and of his Christ."

Here we might enter upon a more minute examination of the elements which enter into the constitution of a righteous civil government. For these, however, we refer the reader, as well as for the application of the principles which we have vindicated, to the pages of the *Two Sons of Oil* adding, only, that no government can claim to be in accordance with God's moral ordinance, which does not in Christian lands, honor God in Christ, adopt his law as supreme, regard the rights and privileges of the entire community, particularly of the most needy, which does not deny its bounties to the open enemies of Christ, and direct its operations to the advancement of moral order and the glory of God, in the maintenance of God's law, the support of religion and the restraint of those who do evil against both tables of the Decalogue. These are not "high and ultimate attainments." They are primary and fundamental principles. We do not demand absolute perfection; but we do demand of any government that asks our conscientious support, that it "kiss the Son," that it put itself under that law which only needs to be understood and applied to reach every interest of social life, and every element of moral order, that it trample upon none of its subjects or citizens, that it regard with interest the special kingdom of Christ, bought with his blood, and cherished as his peculiar possession. In this way, and in this way alone, can we vindicate with effect God's ordinance of magistracy, and perpetuate its claims to future generations, and so secure for them the rich heritage of Christian institutions, and the favor of the Most High. Adopting these views, we must withhold, for reasons which are so well stated in this book, our conscientious allegiance from the government of our land, endeavoring, in the mean time, while we labor for a reformation, to demean ourselves as becomes the subjects, disciples, and witnesses of Jesus Christ—the King of kings, and the Lord of lords—the Savior of his body the church.